CW01678206

Thursday's Child

WINSOME
MICHELMORE

Published by
THE AUTHOR

First published 1985.
© 1985 Winsome Michelmore.

All rights reserved. No part of this publication may be reproduced, stored in a retrieval system, or transmitted in any form or by any means, electronic, mechanical, photocopying, recording or otherwise, without the prior written permission of the copyright owner.

TO MY FAMILY

ISBN 0 9510403 0 8

Designed and typeset by Allset Composition, London
Printed and bound in Great Britain by
A. Wheaton and Co. Ltd, Exeter

Foreword

Thursday's child, as the author of these memoirs tells us, has far to go; and how far Winsome Michelmore has gone, far in miles, in her journeyings from land to land, far also in the gathering of a rich store of experience and in her searching of the deep things of life. And now she has enhanced the richness of all she has known and done by setting it down in a style which is as vivacious and colourful as she is herself in her 91st year. Here are reminiscences which shine with no borrowed light, but glitter like the jewels from Tutankhamen's tomb. Here are endless beautifully detailed touches, as the author, advanced in years but with the mind of a bright girl, remembers not only her friends but her frocks. The trenchant tongue of the child in Tasmania has become the trenchant and eloquent pen of one whose mind is a feast of memories.

And oh, what a tale! Daughter of a bishop, young sister of one of our greatest military commanders, she has seen life in all its moods, serene and sombre, lonely and laughing. Through it all she has maintained a serene faith, so that gratitude for all that she has been given shines over the whole story. Wherever she has been, she has served, a habit inculcated early in life. Is that her secret? All those who share in her life through these memoirs will be forced to conclude that fidelity and service bring deep satisfaction. I am honoured to have been asked to write this foreword, and hope that many will find profound enjoyment, and much more, through their reading of this book, savouring its atmosphere, from fabled pre-1914 to the present day, having their own gratitude for life many times multiplied.

The Very Rev. R. M. S. EYRE M.A.
Dean of Exeter

In my uniform. 1915

I

I remember, I remember the house where I was born, so goes the old rhyme, and I do remember the house where I was born. It was Bishopscourt, Hobart, so called because it was the home of my father who was Bishop of Tasmania. I could go all over the house now. It was a large old redbrick house with a big porch over the front door and a verandah all round it. I could go into the kitchen, I remember that well, and my mother's little boudoir, as it was called in those days. The big, cosy nursery was upstairs, full of children of all ages.

To go back to my birth, my mother wanted another girl. She had so many boys already and Una was the last girl, born six years before. So she wanted a girl and said she was to be called Winsome. She also wanted her called Maud and as these names do not go well together they decided to have me christened Maud Winifred, but I would be called Winsome.

I was born in the morning of St. Valentine's Day 1895, a Thursday, 'a Thursday's child has far go to.' I am told that I had a lot of black hair, which my godmother said was like a velvet cap.

Being wanted, I was much loved and made a pet of by my brothers. All my memories of these early days are pictures, no words. I see myself cuddled up in Harold's arms on the sofa, crying because I had toothache, no doubt I was cutting a tooth. I see myself on the lawn with Donald gathering up my curls with a hairpin borrowed from Mother and threading them with daisies.

Later, in 1901, when we came home to England for Father to take up a very big job, I remember the same brother taking me up on deck at bedtime and saying, 'There you are Winsome, look at the Southern Cross, it is the last time you will ever see it.' And it was, for I never again went further East than Suez.

Desmond was born fifteen months after me, so was really like my twin as we were brought up and did everything together. He was a beautiful boy with a crop of dark curls. Later, I should think at about the age of nine years, he learn to play the violin. I remember an occasion when he was taken to London to play in quite a big concert. Mother went with him, of course, but not me. Nevertheless we were all very excited about it. Years ago I met someone, at a friend's house, who told me that she had known Desmond's music mistress who had said to her one day, 'If Desmond Montgomery had lived, he would have been a concert violinist.' But Desmond died at the age of thirteen from a mastoid abscess, which turned to meningitis. That happened when we lived in Chiswick. He went to Colet Court, which was the preparatory school of St. Paul's where my three elder brothers went, Donald, Bernard and, later, Colin.

When Desmond and I were children we did everything together, as I have said. When we were in Hobart, we did not know what snow was like, to us it was just a white cap on the top of Mount Wellington, so we told the older boys how much we would love to see the strange white stuff. One day Harold told us that he and the others were going for a day's walk up the mountain and would bring us back a snowball. They came back with a very big, hard snowball. We were thrilled and took it out to the kitchen to show Cook, who, I think, had never seen snow before either. She put it in a big soup plate and we went off to bed chattering about it. Next morning we went down to the kitchen early to look at it and found only a deep plateful of water. What a disillusionment!

We had a very happy life at Bishopscourt. I was intensely shy, I used to hide behind Mother's skirts and utterly refuse to be photographed. One day Mother hit on an idea. She said, 'Will you hold up Dolly and I will take her photograph?' I gladly did that and somewhere there is a photograph of me, aged about three, in a long dress and holding up a little doll! I wish I could find that photograph.

I have not told you much about my mother's activities apart from being a Bishop's wife with a large family and lots of

Bishopscourt, Hobart.

entertainment of clergy and their wives. She was a great horsewoman. Where she learned and who taught her I don't know, but certainly it could not have been until she went to Tasmania. She had two lovely black mares, Zoe and Phyllis. These she either rode or drove in a light trap, singly or in tandem.

The only one of her children who inherited her love of horses was Harold. He became a very good rider and won all the races and gymkhanas, which stood him in good stead when he went to South Africa at the end of the Boer War. The war was over six months after the Tasmanian Light Horse, which was what he was in, arrived, but he refused to leave South Africa and joined the Police Force, which he loved. Later he realised that there was not much future in it, so he read law. Later still he moved up to Kenya where he entered the Colonial Service, starting as Assistant District Commissioner, progressing to District Commissioner, then Provincial Commissioner and finally Chief Commissioner for Native Affairs. He was made a Companion of the Order of St. Michael and St. George to my father's joy as he, Father, was Prelate of the Order.

But I am wandering from the subject of my parents, when

Desmond. 1905

Desmond and I were small, in Hobart. Father was sweet to us. In the evenings before bedtime he would put us one on each knee and read to us a big book called 'The travels of Miss Jones, Miss Brown and Miss Robinson'. How we loved it, and he would take off his episcopal ring, which was a seal ring, and press it on our little fat arms to make its mark. I remember that so well. In those days children did not call their parents 'Mummy' and 'Daddy' as they do now. We called ours 'Dada' and 'Mother'. I remember Father coming downstairs at Bishopscourt saying, 'You must not call me "Dada" any more, it is time you called me "Father".'

Mother taught us our letters and how to read. She used a little old book printed on linen in quaint lettering. First the alphabet, then short words, CAT, MAT, RUG, BAG, etc. We first had to learn the alphabet by heart, then graduated to words. I was an avid reader and once I had learned I always had my nose in a book. I remember hiding under the dining table, with its daytime dark cloth over it, reading 'The Little Duke' and crying over it. I was found by Mother and hauled out and given some minor punishment. We were brought up on all Miss Molesworth's books, 'Carrots' etc., and on the Sunday shelf were very goody goody books such as 'Ministering Children' and 'Froggy's Little Brother'. Sunday, for Desmond and me, was not a miserable day as I believe it was for the older boys. We enjoyed it, we liked going to the Cathedral in the morning, we slept all through the sermon, leaning up against Mother, and in the afternoons we were allowed to take out all the Sunday books and also to paint pictures, in a big, bound copy of a publication called 'Sunday'.

We used to go away once a year to a place on the coast called Governor's Bay and we used to see snakes in the garden and enormous tarantulas, as big as dinner plates.

I was a very rude little girl, I fear. One day I was busy making mud pies in the drive just inside the front gate, when an acquaintance of my mother's passed. 'Oh, you are a dirty little girl. What would your mother say?' she remarked. I looked up and said, 'My mother would say, "Go away rude lady and don't interfere with other people's children".'

2

We had to leave Tasmania in 1901, when Father was sent for to become Secretary of the Society for the Propagation of the Gospel. We went to live at Bishopsbourne in Chiswick.

To begin with, Desmond started his education with me under the tuition of Miss Lawrence. We gathered in a few more local children and had quite a little school. Miss Lawrence gave us, I think, a well balanced education. Colin had been born six months before we left Hobart and had a nurse who also looked after Desmond and me. One day when we were out walking in Chiswick High Road, Nurse suddenly stopped, saying, 'Oh look children, there is a motor car!' And there it was! Such a strange thing, all made of brass with big wheels. We went home in great excitement to tell Mother. I can see the baby Colin in his pram now. He wore quite a large cream silk hat, trimmed with white ostrich feather tips and tied under his chin with cream satin ribbon!

Desmond's death in 1909 was my first big grief and one I can never forget. We had done everything together and we loved each other. We were all with him when he died. He had high fever with scarlet cheeks and with his lovely dark hair he looked so beautiful lying in Mother's arms, unconscious. Then he struggled to get up. Mother and the nurse helped him and he opened his eyes very wide, gazing at something. What? We all wondered. That beautiful boy certainly saw something. Next morning I wanted to see him again. He looked like a marble statue. I was crying bitterly and remember Mother putting her arm around me and saying, 'Poor darling, it is worse for you than for any of us for you have lost your mate.' After that the relationship between me and Mother changed. She became more of an elder sister to me than a mother.

I used to confide in her, telling, when I grew older, of my love affairs and discussing clothes etc. with her.

I went to Putney High School when I was thirteen, leaving Colin and Brian to the care of Miss Lawrence. Brian was born at Bishopsbourne, a seven month baby, so small that he had to be kept in cotton wool and covered in olive oil for two months, but he was a beautiful and perfect baby and soon grew up to be a strong boy. He had a crop of fair curls and as Colin had dark curls they were a very striking looking pair, and a pair of little monkeys too! We all loved Colin and Brian.

One very important member of the Chiswick household was Kaffa, short for Katherine. She was our sewing maid and beloved by us all. She came to us from Marlborough College after years of looking after hordes of boys. My Aunt Evelyn, whose husband was the Bursar, suggested that she should retire from Marlborough and come to my mother. She lived in her bedroom with a sewing machine. She wore a long white apron and had a little bun of grey hair and she mothered us all. She must have saved Mother hundreds of pounds for she made, mended and altered. She did everything from sewing on Father's gaiter buttons (bishops wore gaiters and aprons in those days) to making my evening dresses. She loved it when I brought home materials and said, 'Let's plan a new dress.' She did all my packing and unpacking and was a slave of the boys, especially of Brian whom she adored.

Talking of evening dresses reminds me that when I actually bought a new evening dress I always went to John Lewis and never paid more than three pounds. My favourite one was a very pale grey chiffon, very feminine and fluttery. I had a dress allowance of thirty six pounds a year. Shoes bought at Saxone were sixteen shillings and sixpence a pair!

There was the year of the hobble skirt, which year I cannot remember, the skirts were so narrow that it was very difficult to get on a bus and they were very ugly, but we had to wear them and hobble in pain. In the war years (1914–1918) skirts were medium length and fashions did not change much. I think a pretty era was 1920. I went to Canada for seven months that year to be bridesmaid to Donald's bride and the dresses at that wedding were

Desmond (at back), Brian and Colin. 1907

lovely, ankle length skirts. I saw my first ever short frock in 1913 when I went to Switzerland for winter sports with Harold and Bernard. It created quite a sensation.

I did no good at school! I was very stupid and failed in all my examinations, but I was quite happy there and liked netball and hockey, but was no good at tennis. I had several great friends amongst the girls.

I left school to go for a year to a Domestic Economy School at Clapham and I loved the work and was good at it. We girls had to do everything in the way of household work necessary to run a house. I remember the final examinations. Two stand out, the laundry and the cookery. The laundry examination was a bag of mixed dirty clothes. My bag contained a baby's long robe which was a mass of pin tucks, lace insertions, little puff sleeves etc. and a man's stiff-fronted, stiff cuffed dress shirt with stiff collar. The starched parts had to be ironed with a curved polishing iron. Then there was a set of woollen underwear, two pillowcases, with frills, and several handkerchiefs. The cookery was a collection of all sorts of uncooked food and groceries which we were told to use to make a meal. I am glad to say that I passed everything and was given an Honours Diploma.

3

We had to live in England because of Father's job, but every summer we went to Ireland and the older boys and Father joined us when possible. The house was looked after by our gardener and his wife, who lived in a two bedroomed house in the yard. Mary could always open up the home and do rough cooking but the summer 'Going to Ireland' was a big thing! We packed for days. On the day of departure a horsedrawn bus would arrive and we all piled into it, three maids, the baby or babies, a dog, Mother, Father and the rest of the children. Then we drove to Euston where we got into a train for Liverpool which had a pullman carriage reserved for us. It had a long table down the centre and Mother and Father would settle down at one end, with us children and the maids at the other.

At Liverpool we rode in another bus, this took us to the docks where we boarded the 'Comic', the steamer for Derry. It left at night and we always looked forward to the high tea provided for us, some hot dish, tea and huge racks of toast, I remember. It was always rough in the Irish Sea and we were usually sick, but no one minded.

As we came into Lough Foyle we were taken down some stairs into the hold of the ship. The steamer slowed down, a doorway was opened, the hooter sounded, and there was a big fishing boat with Mr. Lafferty and one or two other men who welcomed us home with smiles. A ladder was let down, the boat rocked about, but the men helped us down, maids, dog, babies, all of us. The steamer gave us a final hoot and went on its way, and we were home! There were jaunting cars to meet us at the pier and off we drove to New Park, our house in County Donegal.

Picnic in Ireland.

Every year we were allowed to ask our friends, it was an elastic house. Several beds were put into each room and we often sat down eighteen to meals. Food was cheap, salmon was sixpence a pound if you had the whole fish, which, of course, we needed. We had our own supplies of game and picnics were the order of the day.

One thing I enjoyed very much was the friendship between New Park (us Montgomerys), Malin Hall (the home of the Harveys) and Culdaff House (the home of the Youngs). There was a lot of coming and going between us and I made great friends with Maida Stewart, who was a cousin of the Youngs; indeed she is a great friend still. We used to cycle over, seven or eight of us, leaving early in the morning for a ride of eight miles across the bog roads to arrive at either Malin Hall or Caldaff House in time for a huge breakfast. We took our bathing suits, of course, and revelled in the wonderful beaches of Inishowen and the lavish hospitality shown to us. Naturally they, in turn, used to come to us also.

Another girl friend of mine was Kitty Foster, daughter of a Derry solicitor, who later married a man in the Dorset Regiment. At the present time she is living in Derry, and is still a very dear friend, but alas is too old to come over to England any more. We phone each other often and keep in touch. Maida lives in Sussex and I visited her until I was eighty eight, when I had to say that I was too old to go any more.

I must tell you of the sad end of Culdaff House. It was burnt down by the Sein Feiners in, I should think, 1916 when 'the troubles' began. A gang of men arrived and told Mrs. Young what they were going to do. She came out onto the front steps and called out, 'Boys! If any of you have mothers have pity on me and let me have my son's portrait. He has been killed in France and his picture is all I have of him.' The Irish are a sentimental race and that appealed to them, so they carried the big portrait out for her. She moved to a little home on the beach and later Culdaff House was rebuilt.

That memory reminds me to jump many years ahead to when I became engaged to Godwin, my second husband. He asked me what I had seen of the troubles in Ireland. I told him that we had not suffered personally, had only heard shots at night and, for a time, kept a suitcase packed under our beds; but I had had a first cousin killed in Dublin on what came to be known as 'Black Sunday'. Eight British officers were living in one house with their wives and my cousin was shot as he was shaving, dying a few days later in hospital. Godwin said, 'Oh! my G1 was killed in that house. What was the name of your cousin?' 'Hugh Montgomery' I said. 'That was my G1' said Godwin.

Before I leave childhood days I must tell you my memories of our punishments. Like all children of a big family we were naughty at times and my mother believed in some pretty harsh punishments, such as I am sure children do not have now. Her favourite was to smack us on our bare bottoms with a hair brush! That really hurt and we did not easily forget it. Another was to be put to stand in the corner of the nursery for twenty minutes to half an hour. That was maddening for me, missing out on what was happening in the nursery, and it was very boring but if you had a pencil in your pocket you could always get that out and scribble on the wallpaper, which relieved the tedium.

It was our nurse who carried out the 'put in a corner' one and I will say that we never bore any malice. We knew we had been naughty and that we should be punished. A big sin, like lying, meant being sent to Father and he hated it more than we did, bless him. I always came away from his little talk in floods of tears and full of penitence.

I am afraid that I was the naughtiest child of all. For one thing I was cheeky and that had to be put down. One occasion I remember well, it happened at New Park where we children always had tea in the dining room on Sundays with the grown-ups. One day I was chattering away at the end of the big room, at a smaller table. Mother was talking and she called down in mock severity, 'Winsome, I'm talking.' 'So am I,' I said. There was an awful hush of horror and my mother said, 'Leave the room at once and finish your tea in the kitchen.' I slunk out of the room, terrified; the worst part being to have to tell the maids why I had come!

Summer after summer went by with all of us growing older. Donald left home for Canada in 1907. He went out, after three years at Cambridge, to Vancouver to enter a firm of solicitors. Vancouver was then a small fishing port, but it grew quickly, as did Donald's firm and years later Donald became a partner. Bernard went to Sandhurst and used to bring his fellow cadets over to stay.

Everyone enjoyed the shooting. We did not have a grand shoot with beaters, ours was a rough shoot on our mountain, worked with one dog, a setter. The day before Father planned to go out, the old gamekeeper would come and see him and tell him where the best game lay. Next day Father, and perhaps three or four of the house party, would set off with picnic lunches. Two or three of the girls would go with them and our job was to carry the game sticks. Of course we were trained to be absolutely silent. We would follow a few yards behind the guns, then suddenly the dog would set and everybody would stop. Then there was a whirr of wings as the grouse flew up and the guns blazed. It was never a big bag, two to four brace of grouse, perhaps a few woodcock or snipe, and sometimes a hare. The grouse and other birds were hung on the game stick and given to us girls to carry. We jibbed at a hare as too heavy.

One year Una and Andrew Holden, a friend of Tasmanian days, wandered off into the heather and came back two hours later to announce that they were engaged. Great was the rejoicing and that evening Father wrote up the Game Book with, 'So many grouse, 1 hare and a man!' Una married Andrew soon after and went off to live in Cairo, where Andrew had a big job in the Ministry of Finance. He was very clever and had got a first at Balliol. They were married in Old Chiswick Church and I was one of the bridesmaids. Bernard was one of the ushers and went up and down the aisle with a bunch of service sheets saying, 'Card of the match! Card of the match!' We did not see very much of Una after that. She settled down to a full life and had two babies. Later I went out to see her, but that is another story.

4

The First World War began in August 1914. I was grown up by then and the only thing I wanted to do was to nurse. So I took a First Aid and Home Nursing examination and enrolled in the British Red Cross Society. I was attached to 'London 258' and had those numbers in brass letters on my shoulder strap. I loved my uniform. The dress was a blue grey and I got the laundry to put extra blue into the rinsing water to make it look nicer. There was a white apron with a big red cross on the bib and a white veil cap. Over this I wore a warm, dark blue overcoat which I had lined with scarlet. I do not know if that was regulation, but I got away with it.

My first assignment was to the Duchess of Rutland's Hospital for Officers in Arlington Street, just a few yards from the Ritz. I was to be on night duty, reporting at 8 p.m., and I arrived just after the air raid warning went, there was a Zeppelin overhead. I rang the bell and the door was opened by the Duke who said, 'Come on down to the cellar!' There I found the Duchess, their daughter Lady Diana Manners (later Cooper) the celebrated London beauty, a nurse or two and some patients. Other patients not fit to leave their beds were up in the wards with a Sister and other nurses.

I cannot remember how long I was at the Nursing Home but I learned quite a lot about nursing. I was put on day duty after three months and I had a gay time as the patients who were near discharge were allowed out at night and used to ask me and the other young nurses to dinners and dances. Bernard took a hand in these evenings when he was on leave and used to sit and watch us dance, and foot the bill. Lady Diana was lovely and wore a fascinating white uniform. She was out a lot, but the family had some very interesting friends who used to come in to see them. They kept a suite of rooms in the hospital. I often met people like Margot Asquith and the Tree family, Sir Beerbohm and his lovely daughter Viola.

After some time at the Rutlands', I was told that I was to go to the Outpatient's Department of the South London Hospital for Women, near the Elephant and Castle. We had to help them out to replace trained nurses who were wanted in War Hospitals. We went to the hospital every day and lived at home. We girls, there were three of us, I think, learned a lot we had never known anything about before. Sister said to us one day, 'You girls are seeing things I have never seen before in all my years of training.' It all passed over our innocent heads and I used to go home in the evening and tell Mother all about it. She listened in fascinated horror. It was all mixed up with ordinary things like tonsils and adenoids, every Tuesday, which meant floods of blood and screaming children. Thursday morning was circumcision, which meant more screaming babies.

After a spell there I was given leave, in 1916, as Father wanted to take me to America with him. He and the Bishop of Worcester were going there to represent England at some Church conference. The Bishop of Worcester took his daughter, so Father took me. We had an adventurous and interesting voyage out as, of course, it was the middle of the war and submarines were about. We were escorted out of Liverpool by two destroyers which did not leave us until we were well out to sea. As we neared America we went through fields of beautiful icebergs. Also, for one frightening day, there was a very thick fog and we had to go very slowly, with the fog horn blowing eerily. Another day we went through the Newfoundland fishing fleet. A biggish trawler, the mother boat, lay quietly with a lot of little boats out all around her fishing all day, until the evening when they would take their catch to the big boat. One man shouted out to us, 'Is the war over yet?' 'No,' said our Captain and threw him down a bundle of newspapers.

Of course I loved my time in the States. We went to Washington and stayed with the Bishop who was a widower and had a daughter with whom I made friends. Father preached in the Cathedral and dedicated a new part of it. From Washington we went to Mount Vernon and visited the lovely home where George Washington died. We stayed in Baltimore and Princeton, both times with friends that Father had made when he went out before, taking my sister Una. I did not see much of Father as he was busy travelling round to various cities, but I had a lovely time with all those friends. Father and they wanted me to stay over Christmas, but I got very homesick because the war was going badly and at least three of my boyfriends had been killed. America was not then in the war and my friends could not understand how I felt when I received letters from home telling me about it. So, I asked my hosts to get me a passage home and I arrived back in time for Christmas. I bought my first sleeveless evening dress while I was in Princeton. We went to New York for the day and I bought this pink and silver short evening dress at Macy's, a big cheap store. Mother was a bit horrified at first, but got used to it.

It was then time to go back to work. I was assigned to a Tommies hospital in Kineton, Warwickshire. It got its patients from Birmingham General, mostly men who were nearing the end of hospital treatment. There were some amputation cases etc., but a lot of malaria cases from Gallipoli and Salonika and those were the ones in which I was most interested.

We were worked very hard, having only two hours off duty a day, from two to four in the afternoon, and were so tired that all we could do was to go to the off-duty room, snatch off our caps, light a cigarette and relax. How different from today's frequent off-duty hours! We had one whole day off a week and we usually found a friend who was free on the same day and went to Leamington Spa to have lunch in a café. Rationing was in force and strictly adhered to, I do not know how I would have managed without the seven pound biscuit tin that Mother posted to me once a week full of homemade buttered scones with a jar of jam tucked in between. Those scones helped to fill us up on several afternoons.

Towards the end of my time at Kineton, I was in charge of an eight bedded ward of malaria patients. One man, Thomas, had a double infection so that he would have an attack every two or three days. It meant watching his temperature, changing him when he sweated, sponging him and putting on clean pyjamas. One day I was just ready to go off duty, handing over to a new, nervous V.A.D., and was explaining to her what to do. The child was terrified and said that she could not possibly do it. I said, 'Well, he's just about coming up, I don't mind staying on for twenty minutes to see you over the worst.' Then Sister swept into the ward. 'Nurse Montgomery, what are you doing here? You were off duty at two.' I explained that I was just staying on a few minutes to help Nurse So and So, as it was all new to her. 'Just how selfish can you be?' said Sister, 'Go off duty at once and I will see you later.' She did come in later, put her hand on my shoulder and said, 'I wasn't cross with you, my dear, but you must understand that that child has got to learn and how can she when you do the work for her? I am on duty on this floor and will go at once if she needs me to help her. You must learn to delegate and trust others.' I have never forgotten that, my first lesson in delegation, and I was Sister's slave ever after.

Sometime in 1917 the blow fell. Mother wrote to ask me if I could bear to give up nursing and come home to help her run the house at Chiswick. The last maid had left to make munitions and Mother could not cook. Of course I went and I really enjoyed it. In spite of Domestic Training College I was not a very good cook but I soon got used to it; it was fun trying to make the best of the rations and giving the family what they asked for. Also I was at once swept into a whirl of dance invitations and dancing was a passion with me. It seemed as if every day there came a telephone call, 'Will you come out tonight? I've got three days leave, we'll dance at Princes or the Piccadilly or wherever.' Off I would go and find a perfectly turned out, khaki clad young man. Very different to the mud stained boy he must have been a few hours before. We never discussed what they had been doing. It was dreadful when I would see or hear of their deaths. Bernard was so good to me; whenever he could he would find out where my friends where killed or wounded and write to me at once. We did

My mother, in Ireland.

not only go to dances, we went to theatres. I saw 'The Chocolate Soldier' thirteen times and 'Romance', with Owen Nares and Doris Keene in it, six times. Also very popular was another play, 'The Arcadians', and a revue called 'Bizz-Buzz'.

I think I had very understanding and long-suffering parents, for they allowed me so much liberty and gave me a latch key. I suppose some of the young men saw me home but I am pretty sure that sometimes they put me on the train at Waterloo and I came home alone. I can distinctly remember coming through a little garden gate that was near the station, creeping up to the garden door and into the kitchen. How different to the days now, when people are scared of going out at night alone. There was, of course, always talk of the dreaded White Slave Traffic and we would tell each other awful lurid stories of girls suddenly disappearing. Indeed, I remember well hearing of two girls of about fourteen last seen going up in a lift at Harrods and they were never heard of again.

We still went to Ireland all through the war and many serving soldiers came to stay, sent by my brothers for a few days leave. All were made very welcome. My brother Donald joined up in Vancouver and came home to be trained. At one time he was in a camp near Aldershot and he asked me to go and stay at a small hotel as his guest so that I could see him and get to know some of his friends. He later went to France, did well, got his majority and earned a Military Cross. In Ireland, one summer when he was in France, a very tall Canadian came off the Derry bus and announced himself as Leo Buchanan, 'A friend of Monty, he said you wouldn't mind.' He had no one at all that he knew in England. He looked at me and drawled in his Canadian accent, 'Are you the one Monty calls the half-penny newspaper? He says you know everyone in the village and what goes on and you can tell me.' 'What cheek!' I said. I am glad to say that Donald came through without being wounded. He got married to a Canadian girl in 1920; they had a military wedding and asked me to go out and be one of her bridesmaids. But I am going too fast, I had other travels before that.

5

As soon as the war ended in 1918 my father was released from his work for the Society for the Propagation of the Gospel, we sold Bishopsbourne, packed up and went to live at New Park for good. Father had stayed beyond his retirement time because it was difficult to find anyone to replace him. How happy he was then! Free to go and fish for trout in the little Moville river, or to take his gun and get what he could on the mountain. It was his greatest joy to go visiting amongst his tenants and to help the Rector in our little church. This was just outside our garden and had been built by one of our great uncles.

I too was happy. My parents had an idea that I was not going to marry, as I had refused several men, so they settled a little money on me, not much but enough for me to dress on and to enable me to go over to England and visit my friends. A little room, known as the Den, next door to the drawing room was given to me for my own sitting room. There I would have my friends to tea. We would perhaps take the pony and trap and go for a drive, then come back and toast baps in front of the fire. This made me feel very independant.

There were lots of men I liked very much but with none of these did I get that very necessary spark. Mother would say to me, 'Winsome, are you going to marry So and So?' 'No.' 'Then you must not continue to go out with him, as he is obviously going to propose.' She was a wise old lady, my mother.

Very soon after the end of the war, at the very end of 1918, Una wrote to my mother and asked her if she would allow me to go to Cairo and look after a baby she was expecting shortly. For some reason the doctors had told her she would have to

New Park House, Moville, Co. Donegal.

stay in bed for two months following the birth of the child.

With my agreement, Mother said, 'Yes.' It was very difficult, almost impossible in fact, for any civilian to get a passage on a boat to the East, but Father had a great friend, Lord Inchcape (he always called him the Inchcape Rock), so he wrote to him, told him the story and asked if he could somehow get me out. To my joy, he got me a passage on a troopship which was going to India, which would drop me off at Port Said. I shared a cabin with some woman, either a wife of one of the soldiers or a nurse, I do not remember which.

I arrived three days after the baby was born, another girl named Irene Rose. The nurse said she would stay on for a week or so until I had settled down and got into the way of looking after the new baby and also my sister. She could not stay long herself as every trained nurse was badly needed in the hospitals, which were crammed with soldiers all wanting the final stages of nursing before being sent back to their respective countries.

At last, after a week or so, I was left in charge. Curiously enough the baby never became 'my' baby. The one I loved was Sheila aged eighteen months, not pretty but quaint like a little fair haired gnome. She got into my heart straight away and she has been there ever since, the daughter I never had. Every day, after the two o'clock feed and settling Una to her afternoon sleep, I used to put the baby in her pram and hand her over to the English nanny who looked after the two elder children. Then I put Sheila in her push chair and took her for a walk in the garden of the Gezira Club, hoping people would think I was her mother!

At seven o'clock my work was done for the day and I used to change and go out dancing. I suppose Andrew, my brother-in-law, must have introduced people to me for I soon made some friends and had a very good time. I left Andrew to heat Una's Benger's and to give the baby to her for the ten o'clock feed. I went out dancing four nights a week to Shepheards Hotel, The Continental, the Gezira Club or to Mena House Hotel, close by the Pyramids and the Sphinx. Very romantic on moonlit nights! Andrew took me to the Museum several times to see the wonderful things recently discovered in Tutankhamen's tomb. Wonderful jewellery just like our jewellery of today, gorgeous necklaces of lapis lazuli and amethysts, most beautiful needlework done on very fine linen with pintuck gathers and even feather stitching. Truly, 'There is nothing new under the sun,' we have not progressed at all.

In April we all left on leave. There was trouble in Cairo, I do not know what about, but a friend of mine, a Major in the Duke of Cornwall's Light Infantry, was very worried about us and insisted on sending his large car with a soldier driver to take us to the station, many of us. At the station we found shutters down over all the windows, but we got to Alexandria safely and on to the old 'Kaisar-i-Hind', a P. & O. boat. There was a mixed lot of passengers including both civilians and army officers. We arrived in England in a snowstorm and must have looked rather odd in panama hats with chiffon veils hanging down below our necks.

We spent most of that summer in Ireland or in Dorset, which was Andrew's home, and then the Holden family went back to Egypt, Una being quite strong again by now. During this time Donald had become engaged to his Vancouver girl, Dorothy Waghorn, and asked me to come out to Canada to be one of Dorothy's bridesmaids.

So it was travel again for me. I went at the end of January and it was bitterly cold. In Montreal, where I was to board a train for the long journey across Canada, I saw a house completely covered in thick ice. It had been on fire and the water from the firemen's hoses had frozen where it had fallen! Trains were not air conditioned in those days but grossly overheated and that heat and the smuts were indescribable. The heat took all the curl out of my very curly hair and I remember 'Dodie', as my brother called her, saying, 'Monty has shewn us photos of you with curly hair. What have you done to it?' But a shampoo and a return to normal temperatures soon revived it.

I had a lovely time in Vancouver. The Waghorns made me feel one of the family and it was such fun getting the newly-weds' home ready and planning the wedding and the bridesmaids' dresses, which were very pretty. There was one other bridesmaid besides me; we wore pale primrose yellow frocks with tiny little frills on the sleeves and skirts. They were married on April 20th and I stayed on until August. This was longer than I had intended, but I caught a chill which turned to pneumonia and I was really quite ill. After another long, swelteringly hot train journey and then a sea voyage I was ill again at home with a slight touch of tuberculosis in one lung. This meant three months in bed before I was declared free.

We now lived very happily at New Park. We had come down to one maid, usually a girl from the village or from one of the cottages up the hill. The gardener's wife would come in and give a hand with any extra cleaning.

Brian was now at Sandhurst and became a near and a very good companion for me, although he was nine years younger than I. We went to all the Derry dances together, sometimes staying the night either at the Deanery or the Palace, both families were friends of ours. Or, if it was not a very late dance, we would catch the last late night bus which would put us down at the front gate. On such occasions we would creep into the kitchen, heat up milk and add potcheen (illicit whiskey) into it. This was given to us by the gardener's wife and I shudder to think what our parents would have said if they had known, but they were sound asleep upstairs.

It was through Brian that I met Wangy, my first husband. I had gone over to England in the autumn of 1922 to visit some old friends. Fares were so cheap it meant nothing, about ten pounds return. While I was there one of the Malin Hall girls wrote to me saying, 'When are you coming home? The new regiment, The Royal Sussex, are really nice.' So home I went and after Christmas the dances began. We reckoned on going to fourteen in the Christmas holidays, some at private homes, some public ones in the Guildhall, such as the Rugger and Hockey Club Dances.

One day Brian said, 'John Bellamy wants to know if his mother can write and ask you to a dance she is giving for him.' John was the son of the commanding officer of the Royal Sussex and was at Sandhurst with Brian. I said, 'Nonsense Brian, I'm much older than John and his friends. He doesn't really mean it.' However they persisted, Mrs. Bellamy wrote to me and I accepted and went. Here is the extraordinary part. Mrs. Bellamy went to Wangy, Captain Holderness, and said almost the same words to him. He replied, 'Nonsense Mrs. Bellamy, you don't want an old man like me.' (He was thirty four.) But Mrs. Bellamy said, 'I do Wangy, for I have some very charming girls coming in from the Free State and they are all older than John.' So he accepted, although he was no dancer and very much a bachelor, never going to parties unless he had to.

He and I were introduced to each other as soon as I entered the room. He asked me to dance and it was all up with us. I knew at once that I had met the man I had been waiting for, and he felt the same. This was a thé dansant which were often given then, from four to seven o'clock. I remember I wore a bronze crepe-de-chine dress with elbow length sleeves and a short skirt.

The top was embroidered with little bronze beads and I wore an amber necklace, I had bought the dress at Bourne and Hollingsworth.

I soon discovered that he, Wangy, was a New Zealander and that Wangy was a regimental nickname derived from some New Zealand place. The Regiment was great on nicknames. There was a Head who was 'Beachy' at once and an Oliver who was 'Bath' and so on. As I have said, Wangy never went to dances, so was never on any of the Mess acceptances. He found out that evening which dances I was going to, went the subaltern who had made out the list for the next one and said, 'How many have you accepted for the So and So's dance?' 'Eight, Sir.' was the reply, 'Well put me down even if you have to take yourself out.' When he got there, there was no me. I had not said I was going to that particular dance, as I did not know the family! His rage was great but we met at the next one and he booked me for all the foxtrots and twosteps, he could not waltz, and we fell more and more in love.

We had met at the Bellamy's on January the thirtieth. Shortly after that he was sent to Hythe on a gunnery course. Before he went he asked me to go up to Derry to lunch with him, but the day before I woke up with frightful pains in my stomach. I knew something was really wrong and asked Father to write to Captain Holderness and tell him that I was ill and would not be able to come up to lunch next day. Father wrote a short postcard not giving any details. Poor Wangy had been up to the Melville Hotel early, fussing about the menu and the wine etc. and I never turned up. After waiting an hour he returned to the Mess to find Father's card, which had arrived by the second post!

I was so ill that Father got scared and wired to Mother, who was in England, to come home. To cut a long story short, I was seen by a surgeon from Derry who diagnosed an appendix abscess and ordered me up to his nursing home at once. He operated on me late at night and found he could not get the appendix out as it was bound down by adhesions; all he could do was to drain the abscess. He made a very good job of it and told me that when I got quite strong, if the appendix gave any further trouble, I must have it out at once. He did NOT tell me it was tuberculous, but of course he put that in his notes.

When I was better I wrote to Wangy at Hythe, telling him all about it and that I would be in the nursing home for some time. His course was not a long one and he soon came back and was an almost daily visitor. My nurse was a brick. She thought it a wonderful romance and used to tell visitors that Miss Montgomery was not quite so well today, or that Miss Montgomery had had enough visitors for the time being, and all the time Wangy was upstairs with me! I arranged for Mother to meet him one afternoon and he asked her if he could drive me home, which was twenty miles. He came down to New Park the following week, on the eleventh of April, and asked me to marry him. And so we were engaged.

Then he went to his Commanding Officer. 'Sir, I have become engaged to Miss Montgomery. Have I your permission to go into the Free State?' 'No, you haven't, but jolly good luck to you my boy!' was the reply. Officially, no army officers were allowed into the Free State.

We were married the following thirtieth of January, a year after we had met, in our little Moville church, not the big Derry Cathedral, as I was not really fit and anyway we loved the idea of a country wedding. It meant a great many of our friends could not come and none of the Regiment. However, Mrs. Bellamy came and Colonel Bellamy allowed the best man to come, but I do not remember his name. Two irrepressible subalterns, Whistler and McNab, broke all the rules, dressed in old tweed jackets etc., and came down by car. (Whistler ended by being General Sir Lashmer Whistler). Of course they were not invited to the wedding lunch and none of us knew they were there until we left New Park. It was a lovely little wedding. Father gave me away and I was married by the Rector, assisted by the Regimental Chaplain. We had bought my white wedding dress in Belfast. Nowadays I should say it was fussy, but I think it was pretty; ivory satin, the skirt caught up with a big pearly spray, with wide ivory georgette sleeves which had insets of silver lace. Wangy wore morning dress with spats and grasped a pair of gloves. This was early 1924 and we had decided to 'do it properly' – and so we did!

After the lunch we said goodbye and left by car. Then the fun began. The two subalterns left just in front of us and every time we had to stop at a check point, or custom post, they stopped in front of us and pelted us with confetti and added to the tin cans and things hanging on to the car! They escorted us to the railway station where we found Colonel Bellamy and the whole of A Company, which Wangy commanded. The Colonel made me a charming speech, we were seen into our own, reserved, first class carriage, already full of confetti, and went off to the sound of fog signals that had been put on the line.

We had dinner at a Belfast hotel, then got on the Liverpool steamer and next day started off by train for a little place in South Devon called Bantham Sands, near Thurlestone. Wangy had decided to take me somewhere quiet where I could rest and get really strong. I certainly did, and we came home after three weeks to begin my first taste of Army life. Three months in Derry at the Melville Hotel, then A Company was sent to Enniskillen for three months, back to Derry and then back again to Enniskillen. Each time there we lived in a few rooms next to the Mess, which were barely furnished with army furniture that no officer's wife would put up with now. They do not know what Army life was! We did not mind anything. I had to visit the married soldiers' wives and they lived in far worse conditions than we did, just finding rooms where they could.

We had a year or two doing this so Wangy and I were often able to go home to New Park for weekends. My family loved Wangy (by the way, his real name was William) and I introduced him to all the village and took him to all our picnic places. He got to know Bernard and Brian very well.

6

In 1926 the Regiment moved to England, to Bordon in the Aldershot Command. My lung was now giving trouble so Wangy took me to see a first cousin of his, a Harley Street specialist, Dr. Izod Bennet. He said that I had tuberculosis and as he had the old surgeon's notes he knew the whole story. He said at once that I must go to Switzerland for six months, there was no quick remedy in those days.

It was, of course, heart breaking for us but it had to be. Wangy took me out to the English sanatorium owned by Sir Henry Lunn at Montana, 6,000 feet up. The cure was rigorous, bed for two months with wide open windows and the snow blowing in. Then up to measured exercise with temperature taken before and after the walk. If I had not been so in love I would have broken lots of the rules, as many of the silly patients did, but I was determined to get well and I did. I left six months later with my right lung well and truly fibrosed, but I had orders from Dr. Bennet to go on with the prescribed rest hours of ten to twelve o'clock, two to four o'clock and six to seven o'clock, for several years. Actually I kept to them for five years. It meant giving up most of the social life of the Regiment, but I still made a lot of friends and was able to do quite a bit.

After Bordon we moved to Dover which I did not like. The east wind never seemed to stop and I was not allowed out of doors in an East wind! There was a brigade stationed at Dover. The Royal Sussex were at Castle Barracks, just beside Dover Castle which overlooks the Channel towards France. There was another regiment up there also, the Highland Light Infantry. One of the subalterns of that regiment was David Niven, later to leave the army and become a film actor. An amusing story can be told about him. One day the Adjutant came to the Colonel and said that he thought he should know that David was running his car on a Guinness label (the quarterly label that month was exactly the same colour). The Colonel said, 'Send David in to me.' When David arrived, the Colonel said, 'What's this I hear? Look here, you really can't do things like that.' and David said, 'Well Sir, I can't afford to drink beer *and* run a car.'

We lived in one of eight bungalow quarters for officers, a semicircle of them on the cliff behind the Castle. The Brigadier at that time was Sir Hereward Wake always known, of course, as 'Hereward the Wake'. Wangy and I, on our walks with our beloved white, rough-haired terrier, Derry, used to get great amusement from watching the Dover to Ostend boat ploughing about in the rough seas. Wangy did well. He got a Brevet which helped him on with his promotion and that meant he was next on the list to command the Depot, which was at Chichester.

We moved there in 1933 and that began the happiest time of our army life. The barracks at Chichester are about a mile from the centre of the town, up North Street. They are behind a long wall with the Guard Room at one end. Inside is a large green grass square with the Orderly Room and Regimental Sergeants' Mess one side and the Officers' Mess and Commanding Officer's quarters the other. These, the Mess and Commanding Officer's house, were quaint old cottages built by French prisoners in the Napoleonic wars and were very attractive. Behind us was the N.A.A.F.I. and the Garrison church and all the troops' barracks were at the end. So we were all enclosed together and all Wangy had to do was to leave the front door and walk a few yards to the Orderly Room or take parades on the green in front of us. He frequently got up early, was dressed in uniform by six a.m. and out to inspect parades and so on. We lived by bugle calls, I knew them all and could almost tell the time of day by them.

I had fun getting curtains and carpets made to fit the little rooms and I advertised for a cook general and got one well recommended by a trio of sisters, the Misses Frisbys of the big shoe firm in Lancashire. Her name was Mary. She had been kitchen maid to the Frisbys' cook, who left a lot to Mary, having taught her well. On dinner party nights, Mary told me, Cook would instruct her what to do and not appear in the kitchen herself until six p.m. Consequently Mary was a treasure. She wanted to be in a place of her own and she was delighted to come to us for the sum of £36 a year. She not only did the cooking but also the house work. She would turn down our bed at night and lay out my long evening dress or skirt, for in those good old days we dressed for dinner however simple a meal it was. Wangy wore a dinner jacket and he kept two going, one for home wear, an old one, and one for parties and going out. He, of course, had a batman who looked after his clothes, acted as valet, waited at table and answered the front door bell and telephone. Looking back on it, it all seems like a world of luxury. The batman had all his meals with Mary, who loved army life and soon made up her mind that she would like to marry a soldier, have a daughter and call her after me. It all came true.

One day I said to Wangy that it seemed rather hard luck that Mary could never see a Church Parade and would he mind if we had a cold lunch on Sunday so that Mary could go to the 10.30 service. 'Of course,' he said, so I told Mary to change into something nice after breakfast and go and sit next to one of the corporals' wives with whom she had made friends, the married families' quarters were close to ours. There happened to be a new corporal that Sunday. He said, out of the corner of his mouth, to the man next to him, 'Who is the girl across the aisle?' His friend said, 'The Commanding Officer's maid. I'll introduce you in the Corporals' Mess on Tuesday night.' They met and they liked each other and I was told a lot about Padgy Moore. Much later on they became engaged and got married and eventually they did have a daughter and they did call her Winsome!

While we were at Chichester we were invited to several large dinner parties. One of the hostesses was Lady Cable, who had a very famous chef. Her parties were a delight. I remember once, the chef made a big swan of spun sugar for a spectacular pudding course. It shone like glass and the swan's back was filled with crystallized fruits of all sorts and sizes, all made by himself of course. At one of Lady Cable's parties I sat next to General Sir Ivo Maxse, a dear old man who evidently enjoyed food for, as we sat down and he looked at the menu, he said to me, 'Eight courses my dear. This is going to be a pre-1914 dinner. Do you think you will eat every course?' I regret to say that I did. The courses were not all big ones though; one, for instance, was just asparagus.

The biggest and most spectacular dinner party to which we were invited was at Petworth House in Sussex, the home of Lord and Lady Leconfield. Every three years Lord Leconfield gave a big dinner for the three armed services. Each service had its most senior officer as the chief guests. The only one I can remember is Sir Roger Keyes, representing the Royal Navy.

When the invitation arrived we knew that we were in for big stuff as it said, 'White tie, medals and decorations.' That meant long white gloves for me. Gloves in those days were worn on all state occasions. Long, white, fine kid gloves with tiny little buttons, either eight or twelve according to length. For the Petworth dinner I had a dress of black panne velvet with shoulder straps and a low, heart shaped neck. The skirt ended in a tiny little train and I had very long white gloves coming well above my elbows.

Wangy said, 'I'm damned if I'm going to drive our own car to Petworth House, dump you at the front door and then go and park it. We'll hire one.' So that is what we did and arrived in style. We were met by liveried footmen at the door who took our coats and showed us the table seating plan in the hall. Then we went up a long staircase and were announced by name to Lord and Lady Leconfield who were standing at the top. We then joined the other guests in the Long Gallery where we had drinks and chatted to people before all going into dinner.

There were two tables, Lord Leconfield was at the head of one and Lady Leconfield at the head of the other. Lord Leconfield's had gold plate, every plate and dish made of gold and Lady Leconfield's had silver. I had only seen its like at the Mansion House in London, where I once went to a big dinner with my father as my mother was ill. Each table had as its centre piece a model of some famous battle. I sat at Lord Leconfield's table and Wangy at Lady Leconfield's. I remember that I sat next to an Air Vice Marshal whom we met later on at Remleh when we were in Palestine. The food was lovely of course.

After dinner we women withdrew to the Long Gallery again and listened to the music of a Hungarian band, then the men came in and talked to us. Lord Leconfield gave me a few minutes. He was a dear old man. He told me that he and his wife had no children of their own so they had adopted two. I enjoyed the conversation as I was always interested in adoption. Then when Mrs. Mansel and I were sitting on a sofa and talking, the unmistakeable Lord Hailsham came along and asked if he could sit down and talk to us. That really gave me a thrill. I look at the pictures of the present day Lord Hailsham now and think how like his father he is.

That evening certainly was a memorable one and yet, try how I will, I cannot remember who the Heads of the Army and the Air Force were that year! Memory is a queer thing. I have remembered a lot in these memoirs of mine and yet if you were to ask me what I was doing last week I could not possibly tell you! I suppose that it is a question of things photographing themselves on the brain. They do not make a firm impression when we get old.

Wangy and I had quite a lot of visitors to stay and looking after them was too much for Mary who had dinner to cook. I asked a corporal's wife, who had told me that she had been in domestic service, if she would like to come over when I had a woman visitor, unpack for her, put out her dress and so on and also help the batman wait and clear up. She jumped at the offer so I bought her a dark green cotton dress from Marks and Spencers, a coffee coloured apron and little cap. She looked so nice and it all worked out so well. Believe it or not, I only paid her five shillings for the evening! And she got a tip from the visitor. Those were certainly the days.

Once a year the Depot was 'At Home'. There was a big marquee put up on the Green and a great many people came to an afternoon party. Then, being so close to Goodwood, we had to attend the races there on all three days. We also had to put people up, as did the officers at the Mess next door. There was, and still is, a Royal Sussex tent on the racecourse, where everyone gathered for lunch.

In early 1936 it became clear that Wangy would soon be commanding a battalion and it was thought it would be a good idea for me to be presented at Court. So we set things in train and I was accepted by the Lord Chamberlain. Freda Goring, of the Regiment, said she would present me and would lend me her three white feathers which she had worn at her presentation and her mother before her. Eileen Stirling Hamilton, a Chichester friend, said she would lend me her big fan of flame coloured ostrich feathers instead of a bouquet. The two husbands, Wangy and 'Pope' Goring, were looking forward to a night out in full dress when disaster struck. The old enemy, my appendix, woke up and I was rushed up to the Middlesex Hospital where Dr. Bennet arranged that I should be operated on. At the same time news came that the 1st Battalion was to go to Palestine and that Wangy was to go out as Second-in-Command. These two things meant all plans for my presentation had to be cancelled and I never had another chance. I was sorry about it, but never found that it made any difference.

When the surgeon operated on me he got the appendix out and, joy of joys, found that there was no sign of any tubercle left. I was in the Middlesex Hospital's private wing for some weeks and made an excellent recovery. Margaret, Colin's wife, came down to stay with Wangy while I was away and was a great help to him.

I have not written about Colin and Margaret yet. Margaret was my best friend and we four always got on well together. Wangy and I went to stay with them at their vicarage in Wallasey several times. One year we took Wangy's batman with us and he was a great help in the house. Colin was fun. One day Wangy and Margaret went over to Liverpool to do some shopping, leaving me to look after Colin and cook his lunch. Margaret was due to run a little club she had for mothers in the parish. She usually read aloud to them while they sewed. Colin had impressed on her that she must be back by three o'clock but by then there was no sign of the truants, so Colin said that I must go in her place. I tried to object, but with no success. We went to the Church Hall where Colin opened the door saying, 'Well, my wife has run away with my brother-in-law so my sister has come to look after you.' I did not read to them as all they wanted to do was to bombard me with questions about army life and shortly afterwards a very sheepish-looking Margaret and Wangy returned.

7

The Regiment sailed for Palestine on the day of the Abdication of King Edward VIII. We wives could not go with them as there was trouble in Jerusalem but we were told we would go sometime in the spring. We all saw the ship sail away without us, I, as usual, in floods of tears. Having had a very busy three years at Chichester, I decided that I would like to be on my own, so I took rooms at Southsea, where I was very comfortable. I had my various injections at the Military Hospital. I cannot remember where I spent Christmas, but am sure it was somewhere nice. I found a church I liked and went to it regularly. I read a lot and walked on the sea-front. Often I would get on a bus and go over to Chichester to see my friends. Finally we got word that we could join our husbands and we sailed in March.

Wangy met me at Port Said and took me up to Jerusalem. We, and about seven other officers and their wives, lived in a pension called the Villa Rosemary. We each had a bedroom and a sitting room and we all ate in the communal dining room. Our Chaplain advised us to use H.V. Morton's 'In search of Palestine' as our guide book, which we did. Whenever our husbands were off duty we explored Jerusalem, which was open to everyone then. It had no barriers as there are now. It was an experience I can never forget. The Bible, both Old and New Testaments, came alive as we saw Abraham's tomb, the Pit of Dothan, Rachel's tomb, the Shepherds' Fields and Bethlehem. We saw it all as residents, not as tourists.

Every Sunday, after Church Parade, we would pick up our bathing things and a packed lunch and drive down to Jaffa where we spent the afternoon until about five o'clock. Then we all raced back in our cars so as to be in the city before the six o'clock curfew. Such a dry, dusty road, but it was the road where Jesus must often have walked, the road where he was missing for three days after being in the Temple.

We went on a trip to Galilee and bathed in the lake, then travelled on to Capernaum and to the Dead Sea, where we swam in that awful lake which is so salty that you cannot sink. We went down the road which had an inn called the 'Good Samaritan' then and which seems to be quite likely the road which Our Lord took for his parable. We were in Jerusalem over Easter and saw the Ceremony of the Washing of the Feet enacted and the Ceremony of the Holy Fire, which was most moving.

The Coronation of George VI took place while we were in Jerusalem and there was a big ball at Government House to which we all went. Wangy and I, on another occasion, dined at Government House with the Governor, a little bachelor called Wauchope. I, as senior lady, sat on his right, as Cecil Walden's wife did not come out with us. One day the Regiment trooped the Colour, all part of the Coronation celebrations. There was a bit of trouble at times. We would hear bombs go off at night, very much like Ireland. Then there really was trouble. The Mufti (ruler) ran away and our troops were everywhere with fixed bayonets.

My memory fails me at that point but at some time we came home as Wangy was to go to the 2nd Battalion at Devonport. It was stationed in North Raglan Barracks. I remember that he and I lived at an hotel and that I did not like Devonport very much, not after all the lovely places to which we had been.

I have only mentioned briefly my eldest brother Harold who lived in Kenya. He used to come Home every three years for about three months and, as we were very fond of each other, he gave me a wonderful time. He would write one of his very short letters announcing his arrival: 'Darling Winsome, Home on such and such a date. Meet me Boat Train at Victoria, such and such a time. Your loving H.' Never more than that. I would be at the ticket entrance on tip-toe with excitement, to see Harold running down the platform looking very colonial, wearing a large, double brimmed terai hat. He would sweep me up into his arms and into a taxi exclaiming, 'Look at the skirts. How short they are!' Or, another year, 'How long they are!' or 'What are you all doing with your hair?' and so on. Then off we would go for a few weeks of fun.

He was very keen on boxing and used to go out most nights to watch all the big fights in London. He belonged to two clubs, the Overseas and the Sports Club, I expect that is where he got his information about boxing. He was also a gambler and bet on every race. He used to say to me, 'If I win the Lincoln I'll take you to Paris for a week,' but he never did and we never went to Paris although we did go to the Imperial Hotel at Torquay where we had a grand time. He hired a car and we drove over Dartmoor and danced at night.

He was a confirmed bachelor and never bothered about women but at Torquay there was a very nice, very rich, girl staying with her parents who were diamond 'kings' from South Africa. He became interested in her and asked her to dance with him once or twice so that I wondered if I was going to lose my bachelor brother, but I am sorry to say that nothing came of it.

He did finally marry in 1929, a lovely Canadian girl, Ursula Johnson. She had married a cousin of ours, Neville Montgomery, who was killed in the first World War and as a young widow she came to stay with us at New Park at a time when Harold was on leave.

Bernard, the third eldest, was an equally dear brother, but in a quieter way. He used to give me presents from time to time and take me to theatres. The famous story of the hat he gave me once is described in Brian's book, 'A Field Marshal in the Family', and he also once gave me an exquisite pale yellow chiffon blouse from an exclusive shop in Piccadilly. When I became engaged to Wangy, I was surprised and delighted to receive a box of a dozen beautifully embroidered handkerchiefs from the White House in Bond Street, the only engagement present I had. But Bernard's eyes and thoughts were always on the army. A dedicated soldier going on from strength to strength until he ended up as a Field Marshal, known to all the world as 'Monty'.

Just before the first World War, when he was stationed at Shorncliffe, he had me down for a week, asking his Company Commander, Captain Tomes, and his wife if they would put me up. It was very nice of them all and I was glad of it in the future as it gave me a chance to get to know some of his regiment, the Royal Warwickshire Regiment. Now I often meet some of the Regiment as several officers and their wives have retired to Devon. I have made great friends with a number of them and can tell them whom I used to know in the faraway past.

During the three months we spent in Devonport, Harold's wife Ursula contracted cancer in Kenya. She had had it for some time before she told Harold, because she was a Christian Scientist, and things were really bad by the time she told him. Harold was distraught and immediately brought her and their little boy of five, Gardner, called after a Canadian uncle, home to England, saying that he was going to get the best advice and treatment. Ursula would have none of either. She insisted on going to the Christian Scientist Nursing Home, where she very soon died. My mother gathered up Gardner and took him off to New Park, she was so happy to have him and he adored his Granny. Harold was not happy about the arrangement and thought that my mother was not capable of looking after a small boy, he was not at all a good parent, and asked me whether I would have him as my ward. Of course I was thrilled. I had no child of my own and had always wanted one. I could not have him at once so we left him with his Granny for a while.

8

One day Wangy came to me to say that he had just been told that he was to command the 1st Battalion, his own battalion of the Regiment, which had gone out to Egypt. He was very excited about it and so was I except for one thing. I hated the thought of not being able to have Gardner. But it had to be, I could not possibly have him in Egypt. He stayed on at New Park where he and Granny had a grand time, no schooling though!

Wangy went off to take over command and I busied myself buying curtain material and collecting what household things I would want, and finally sailed for Port Said to a very different life from any other I had had. For one thing we were suddenly well off! Pay in the British Army was very poor in those days, as a Major, Wangy only had £500 per year and I had become quite used to being careful. All that ended. Wangy met me saying I was to have what I wanted and we would entertain and really enjoy ourselves. I got our Indian dhirzis (tailors) to make up curtains and bed covers. We had a nice big bungalow but it was not very well furnished. The beds were army beds which cannot be called pretty! I had our dhirzi make covers to go over the bedheads, with bedspreads to match and the result was good. Furniture was mostly cane, no carpet, all tiled floors because of the heat. I had been busy with dressmakers before I went out so arrived with quite a trousseau. How different life was. The lovely sun, the native servants and having to learn to speak to them in pidgin English mixed up with as many Arabic words as I could manage. I had a very good cook called Ibrahim, a 'boy' called Moussa and a little dogsbody, known as a 'wallid'.

We gave a small dinner party once a week, perhaps a couple of subalterns and a young married couple, and a big dinner party once a month for twelve or so. As well as our own companions in the Regiment, there was another Regiment in the camp, also the officials of the Suez Canal Company. I have never said where we were! It was at Ismailia on the Suez Canal and the camp was called Moascar. When I arrived the Essex Regiment was there but it was soon replaced by the Cameron Highlanders, with whom we got on very well, as did the troops. Sussex men seemed to like the Scots.

Altogether we were at Ismailia for two and a half years. Wangy had one company in Cyprus and used to go and inspect them, staying for a few days. I did not go with him, it was better for him to stay in the Mess. Ismailia is exactly half way between Port Said and Cairo, fifty miles from each, and being right on the Suez Canal we saw all the liners and huge tankers going through. One day we actually saw an enormous harbour being towed out to Singapore.

There was a beautiful beach with very good bathing and lots of little beach huts where everyone congregated in the afternoons. We would have a siesta after lunch, then pick up a tea basket from the hall which Moussa had packed. We would get in the car and drive down to the beach and spend a couple of hours there very happily. Some people reading this might well ask whether our husbands did any work! Indeed they did, their day started at six o'clock and they worked very hard. All the officers, Wangy especially, had to be ready for anything at any time.

The transport sergeant wanted to teach me to ride in the riding school but Wangy would not allow it. He said that no one over forty could learn to ride well. I learnt to swim at over forty and believe me it was not good swimming! One day we were all in the water when a cry went up, 'Sand storm coming!' We looked round and there it was, a yellow cloud racing towards us. Immediately everyone dashed to shore and the safety of the beach huts. Owing to the hardening of my right lung I could never run. Wangy urged me on but I could not. All I could do was to motion him on and the sand storm caught me up so that I was covered with it. Wangy waited for me with everything ready and said that I looked as if I was covered with demerara sugar. He hosed me down with water then, after some hot tea, drove me home and I had a bath and suffered no ills.

We wives also got up early in the morning. I made great friends with the wife of a major in the Cameron Highlanders, Eve Duncan. She and I used to meet at six o'clock and ride round the camp on bicycles so as to get some exercise before it got too hot. We did have a spell of cold weather between, I suppose, November and February.

Wangy had promised me that as soon as I knew I had the custody of Gardner I should go home every July when the heat really did become very intense. I loved those holidays and getting to know my new little boy. We would stay with various friends, especially with Colin and Margaret. He told me that he hated his name, Gardner. I quite agreed that it was an awful name so suggested that we should change it to Gary. That pleased him and he has been Gary ever since. We arranged for him to go to a preparatory school, spending holidays with Margaret and other people and, as I say, the summer holidays with me.

I must tell you a few things about my housekeeping in Egypt. It was really very easy for we had a good cook and there were good shops with excellent food of all sorts. Fish caught in the Great Bitter Lake were wonderful; dover soles, halibut etc. and, of course, huge prawns. Every cook loved making prawn curry. Wangy used to say at lunch time, when he saw what was going back to the kitchen even though we had had two helpings each, 'It's easy to see someone else likes prawn curry besides ourselves.' Drink from the N.A.A.F.I. was so cheap. Whisky was seven and sixpence a bottle and gin five shillings! Every evening after our afternoon on the beach, a bath and dressing for dinner, we would sit out on the verandah with large whiskies and sodas.

The Nile Storage Company was rather like one of our superstores, well suppplied with frozen foods. On one occasion we were going to have rather a special dinner party and Wangy told me to go to them and choose something really good and unusual if I could. I found that they had just got a whole scotch salmon so I ordered that to be sent up. Ibrahim evidently had a fish kettle but we had no serving dish large enough and I had to ask the help of the Mess Sergeant. He lent me a large silver plated dish and our guests' surprise and pleasure were nice to see as Moussa proudly handed it round, all nicely sliced.

The climate was not always good; far from it. We had days of sand storms when every window and shutter had to be tightly closed. That meant dark rooms and however tightly the windows were fastened the sand drifted in and got all over the furniture. Then the flies were dreadful. Every afternoon after lunch before we went for our siesta Moussa would go into the sitting room, shut the windows and spray the whole room. When he opened up again he had to sweep up piles of dead flies.

Besides learning a little kitchen Arabic I had to learn to cope with two things: 'squeeze' and 'graft'. Any army officer's wife who may read this knows about 'squeeze'. It is what you had to allow the cook when you paid his daily account, submitted to you when you went out to the kitchen after breakfast to give the menus for the day. 'Lemoons (lemons), so much.' 'Oh Ibrahim, too much for lemoon.' 'No lady, plenty lemoon for lemoon soufflé and much lemoonade.' You always had to allow them their extra bit of money, otherwise you would lose your cook. All the cooks were Sudanese and it was pure luck, plus personal recommendation, before you could get a good one. We had, in the Regiment, a young Captain's wife whose cook was better than the one the Brigadier's wife had.

'Graft' was another thing. Natives always tried it on. One day I was in the drawing room and there was a knock at the door and in came Moussa with a large live turkey under one arm! It was the most ludicrous sight to see this bird with its long neck and beady eyes. I said, 'What have you got there, Moussa?' Moussa said, 'Rahman (the camp contractor) send Colonel's Lady big fine turkey.' I said, 'I don't want a turkey, take it away.' 'Oh, but Lady can give big dinner party and it is a present. I make fine dinner party.' I was adamant and told him to take it away and tell Rahman I did not want it. When Wangy came back for lunch I told him about it as a great joke. He quickly said, 'You didn't take it?' I said, 'No, of course not,' and he said, 'Thank God for that. The old rascal Rahman has been on at me for week to get the contract for bicycles for the whole Battalion and if you had taken his damned turkey I should have had to have given him the contract.'

9

In 1938, Munich year, the sailing of the ship I had booked to go back on after Gary's holiday was delayed by a month. War was beginning to look imminent. So in 1939 I said I would book extra early and leave Gary with some Chichester friends who would take him back to his prep. school in Cheshire for me. I booked a passage for September 14th but, as we know, war was declared on September 3rd. I had left Moville towards the end of August with Gary and we stopped off in Belfast as the 2nd Batallion, which was stationed there, gave a cocktail party for me and we stayed with one of the married couples.

The next night we got on the Liverpool boat and I had just put Gary to bed in the upper berth when there was a knock on the door and in walked John le Mesurier in uniform, he was a great friend of ours. 'Mrs. Wangy, the balloon has gone up. We have all been confined to Barracks but the Commanding Officer has allowed me to come and see you and to ask where you are going and if you will be all right.' I told him we were going to stay with my cousin Hilda Montgomery in Somerset until I sailed for Egypt on the 14th. 'You won't get back to Egypt, Mrs. Wangy, it's war and all sailings are stopped from now on.'

This was awful news, but I was so lucky to be going to such a peaceful spot, a little village called Stocklinch. We heard the Prime Minister's broadcast on Sunday, September 3rd at eleven o'clock in the morning. Hilda was a brick. She said that she was always lonely, had plenty of room in her home and that Gary and I were very welcome to live with her, at any rate for some time.

We were later joined by another cousin, Bridget Lotringa, now St. Germans; her husband was in the Royal Fusiliers and was sent over to France at once. I took Gary back to school myself and then settled down to a time of anxiety like so many others. Bernard was then commanding Third Division and their headquarters were at Crewkerne, not far from us, so we saw him several times. He used to phone and ask himself to tea and I would dash over to Taunton in the morning and buy a Fuller's walnut cake which was a favourite of his.

In time I got letters from Wangy. As soon as war was declared the Regiment was ordered up into the desert and Moascar was taken over by other units. He told me that he only had a very little time in which to leave the bungalow and pack our things. In fact he could only pack what clothes I had left behind and some of the things I had bought and liked, but a very great deal had to be discarded. This included a huge copper tray which I had loved and used as a table as it stood on legs which the regimental carpenter had made for me. Wangy doubted very much whether what he had packed would reach me unbroken and he was right.

I suppose Bridget and I were typical of all soldiers' wives in those days, anxiously looking for letters, which came very rarely, writing often knowing we might not get any replies. We both adored our husbands and talked about them to each other. We usually cried in church, very sentimental we were. Hilda was an angel the way she put up with us. She had a dear little, very old, manor house which was haunted. She had seen the ghost several times and one of the two maids saw it once, but neither I nor Bridget nor Gary ever did.

In time Bridget left us and I settled down and decided that I must find some war work. I found it quite near by with the local Observer Corps. I was on night duty in a big country house called, if I remember rightly, Hinton St. George. I think the house had been taken over by a girls' school from the East Coast and the Observer Corps had their room in the basement. We had camp beds and could rest but we had to be on the alert for any air activity. Nothing ever happened and I found it very boring.

Christmas came with Gary at home. I had got to know several of Hilda's friends and there was a certain amount of mild social

Gary and I in the garden at Stocklinch. 1939

life, but oh! how I missed Wangy and our happy life in Egypt.

Before the Easter holidays I began to think to myself that it was time Gary and I moved on. Hilda was very much a spinster and was used to having her house to herself, so it was noble of her to put with us. She did it loyally for Gary's sake. She was absolutely devoted to him and was his godmother. She was also his aunt as well as a cousin because his mother, Ursula, had been married to Hilda's brother before she married Harold, all very muddling but quite legal.

As I say, I began to think of moving on and was wondering where I could go when out of the blue came a letter from an old friend of mine, Adria Hoare, wife of Wilfred Hoare of Woodlands, Kennford near Exeter, a big house at the foot of Telegraph Hill. It cannot be seen from the road, only the lodge is visible. Adria had a big establishment, several maids and a butler, and she was going through a miserable time as one by one the maids left to go on war work. Finally she wrote to me saying that Fortune, her very nice butler, who had hung on as long as he could, had told her that he must go. She asked if I could bear to come, with Gary, to live with her, Wilfred and her two children and do the cooking. 'I don't know anything about cooking,' she wrote, 'but I suppose I could learn to do some housework.' The only help left was a very nice kitchen maid called Beattie.

This was the answer to my doubts, so we said goodbye to Hilda and went to Kennford. Beattie was a tower of strength. She did all the vegetables and washing up and she and I got on very well. There were plenty of vegetables, eggs, chickens and milk and with all our ration books we fared quite well.

Then our numbers were increased as evacuees descended on us. At first we had a woman and two children from London. They hated the country and begged to be allowed to go back, so they did. Our next lot were boys who immediately took to country life. They went to the village school and, when at home, helped the gardener and the farm man and were very happy. By this time I was cooking for eleven. We had a big Aga stove, so it was quite easy.

It was while I lived with Adria Hoare that I received a telegram from Pickford's at Portsmouth saying, 'We regret to tell you that our store in Swan Street was blitzed last night by incendiary bombs and almost all the furniture stored with us has been destroyed. Can you come and see us?' We had put all the contents of our home in Chichester Barracks in store with Pickford's. Immediately I telephoned Mrs. Southwell, widow of dear Bishop Southwell, and asked her if she would put me up for a night. I took a bus to Portsmouth, arrived at Swan Street and saw a scene of devastation. Masses of soaked and ruined furniture, pictures, pianos etc. A very nice, worried man showed me what was left of ours and the first thing I saw, propped up on the pavement, was a portrait in oils of myself, painted when I was a girl, completely unhurt! It is now in Gary's house in Denver, Colorado.

Next there was some not very badly damaged mahogany bedroom furniture, that had been in our spare room, and some lovely water colours that my father had given to me from time to time as I loved water colours. They were slightly blotched and damp. The worst thing, that made me nearly sick to look at, was a large trunk full of pulped books, so soaked that I could hardly see the titles. I was lucky to see so much saved, I thought. The man said that there was a furniture restorer quite close who could repair the furniture and a picture dealer in the next road who could restore the pictures. I went to see both and arranged for them to get on with the job.

A few days later I got another telegram saying that both shops had been blitzed and all my things were completely lost! I was told that at least three hundred lots of household things had been lost, together with all the names and addresses of the owners, all service people living far away in India, Hongkong etc., so they would never be able to contact them. I was also shown the ruins of a large room where all the pianos had been stored, just a mass of tangled notes and wires.

It was either in these two raids or another quite close that Bernard lost all his things, but it was worse for him because he lost all his wife Betty's lovely pictures and sculptures. One of mine had been painted by her and I had written at once to Bernard and told him I would give it to him, so his raid must have been before ours. Luckily, over the years, various people have given him what they had of hers and they are safe with David at the Mill. For War Compensation we were given £100! I still mourn the books, photographs and, above all, the water colours.

Some time before the end of 1940 Wangy's Command came to an end and he came home to be Chief Umpire, Northern Command which meant he was stationed up at Darlington in Yorkshire. I knew that sometime he would get leave and I was determined that he would find me alone so I told Adria I must go. She took it badly and begged me to stay, saying she would leave me and Wangy alone etc. etc., but I knew it would never work, for I was fully occupied in the kitchen.

I looked around and found rooms in a very nice farmhouse at Powderham called The Red House, on the road to Kenton. It is still there. A Mr. and Mrs. Tuplin owned the farm and they decided to let certain rooms, but not to evacuees of the usual sort, so she was glad to have us. I booked a double room, a single and a sitting room and quite soon Wangy got leave and came down. He only had less than a week but he loved it. Gary came home for the summer holidays but at Christmas we did not want to intrude on the Tuplins, so went into Exeter and stayed a few days at the White Hart Hotel. Wangy had Christmas leave for that.

Adria was a brick. She bore me no malice and our friendship never waned. I believe the faithful Beattie stayed on till the end of the war.

10

As everyone knows, that spring the air raids on the South Coast began. We had German planes flying over us every night on their way to the North. Wangy wrote and asked me if I could go up to Yorkshire as he had got three days leave and he thought we would go and stay at Richmond. Of course I was thrilled and said 'Yes.' Mrs. Tuplin made me up a big parcel of food to eat on the long journey. I had a taxi to St. David's station and when on the platform I noticed a woman of my own age who looked as if she, like me, was going to join her husband. She was, only to somewhere nearer than Yorkshire, but she had to catch the same connecting train at Bristol.

We waited and waited for our train. At last there was a station announcement to say that Plymouth had had a terrible air raid during the night and our train was one and a half hours late. This meant that we lost our connection and we arrived at Bristol to find that it had had a similar air raid. The whole platform was a mass of broken glass, the restaurant was a shambles, there was no gas or electricity and no hot drinks could be had. A porter cheerfully told us that the girl who pushed the sandwich trolley about had been blown to bits.

It was dark when a train came in which they said was going North, so we got into a third class carriage with a lot of Tommies. There were no lights, blackout curtains were pulled across the windows. We all got sleepy. I had a soldier's head on each shoulder. We became very hungry. 'Anyone got any food?' someone asked. I said, 'Yes I have, I'm sure it's good and there's plenty.' I opened up dear Mrs. Tuplin's parcel by the light of a small pocket torch belonging to one of the soldiers and we shared out all the food. Then more sleep. My woman companion raised a laugh when we stopped at a station and heard a porter calling out, 'Chesterfield! Chesterfield!' 'Oh doesn't it sound comfortable,' my new friend said!

We by-passed Sheffield which was being raided and we saw all the anti-aircraft guns in action. Somewhere, I do not know where, I had to change and was put in a troop train for York. Never have I listened to such language!! I felt sick with hunger and all I could find was a bit of chocolate in my pocket. Finally I got to York at 4 a.m. I fell into the Station Hotel, which was mercifully open and said to the night porter, 'Please give me a room and the largest pot of tea you can get with whatever food you can manage.' He took me up to a lovely big room with a private bathroom and brought up a laden tea tray. I was terribly worried about Wangy, who had been going to meet me at 6 p.m. As soon as I could I phoned him and he sounded quite frantic. He had wondered if perhaps I had been killed in one of the raids.

All worries stopped when we reached the peace of Richmond. We stayed at a little pub, we explored the dales, had bacon and eggs for lunch in cottages, walking everywhere. It was bliss. The journey going home was perfectly normal.

Just after that I had pneumonia. The doctor said that Powderham was too damp a place for me. We were on very marshy land which had become flooded and he advised me to find somewhere else if I could. So once again I was on the move and I began to wonder if it was anything to do with 'Thursday's child has far to go'! I had a friend who lived at Henley-in-Arden and she asked me to go and stay with her for a bit until I could find somewhere more permanent.

I had Gary for the Easter holidays and we heard we had missed the terrible blitz of Exeter. Margaret was in Scotland running first a British Restaurant and then a R.A.F. Maintenance Unit. She had a sister in Kirkcudbright with whom she had made her headquarters and this sister, Aileen, said that she did not want evacuees, so would I like to come and live with her and her husband. It was almost too good to be true, not far away from Wangy, quite close to Gary's school in Cheshire and so close to my beloved sister-in-law, Margaret.

We lived there for a year. Wangy came for a couple of short leaves, Gary came for the holidays and Margaret and I were back to our old talking. Colin was Chaplain on a hospital ship. He had given up his parish as he was a territorial in the King's Liverpool Regiment and chose a hospital ship because he loved the sea.

I have quite forgotten to recount a poem that my mother wrote about me and Margaret when I stayed with them for a while in Wallasey, I think it must have been when I was at Southsea. I paid for my board and lodging as they were very hard up. I may have got my dates wrong but no matter, I was with them for some time. This is the poem that Mother wrote:

Winsome and Margaret they talk all day.
What do they talk about? Who can say?
But from early morning to close o' day,
They talk and they talk and talk.

Colin, poor man, is much dismayed.
He looks on and listens, sore amazed.
He humbly asks, 'Can't I talk too?'
But they rudely reply, 'We've no use for you,
When we talk and talk and talk.'

They talk of the weather a bit perhaps,
Of husbands and mothers and maids' mishaps,
Of Mrs. Simpson and Edward VIII,
And they settle all the affairs of state,
While they talk and talk and talk.

When bedtime comes it is just as bad,
And Colin then goes nearly mad,
For Winsome says, as they climb the stair,
'There is something more for you to hear,
I nearly forgot it I declare,
So come to my room while I brush my hair,
And we'll talk and talk and talk.'

Then Mother wrote another poem a year later:

Winsome and Margaret have met once more.
They've been parted, you know, for over a year.
Will they talk as much as they did last year?
Just wait a bit and you shall hear.

Says Margaret to Winsome, 'I greatly fear
We can't talk as much as we did last year,
For Colin, you know, has made me see
That it isn't fair to him and me.'

But Winsome replied, 'What awful rot.
I pay for my board and lodging here
And if I can't talk I shall go elsewhere,
For talking's the only pleasure I've got.'

'Well, but Colin says that the sum you pay
For your board and lodging isn't enough
To pay for the scandal and gossip and stuff
That you talk and talk and talk all day,
So you must pay more or else you can't stay.'

'Well right,' says Winsome, 'I can't afford
To pay any more for my bed and board,
So we'll curb our tongues and I'll stay here,
For I greatly love my brother dear.'

'The weather's a topic that's always safe,
But the Duke of Windsor I fear is taboo
And so are all those with names in "Who's Who",
There's not much more for me and you.'

'But Margaret, one night when Colin is out,
And both the maids are safe downstairs,
To the blazing fire we'll draw up our chairs
And we'll talk and talk and talk.
Oh bother! here's Colin.' 'Goodnight brother dear.'

As I have said, we lived in Kirkcudbright for a whole year, then a great friend of Margaret's, who lived in a village near Farnham in Surrey, asked if Gary and I would go to her for a few weeks.

Colin and Margaret

So, once again, we were on the move.

I found a very nice little flat eventually, just outside Farnham, near Margaret's friend. It had two bedrooms, a little kitchen and a very nice sitting room with a big window looking out onto a wonderful view. We had to share a bathroom with the owner of the house but did not mind. There was a butcher's shop next door and there I got my weekly meat ration, only a few ounces. One week it was a nice large pork chop. I decided to have it on Sunday after church and spent a long time getting ready for it. I cooked a large onion and made apple sauce. I actually made a little stuffing and I had a Sunday lunch fit for a queen.

How did we fare for the rest of the week? Well, we would get an odd sausage or two and we always had dried egg with which we could make scrambled eggs or an omelet. We bought rather dubious pies made of scraps of meat and vegetables and we were greatly helped by parcels from America. My great friend Helen Benson, who lived in Princeton and with whom I had stayed, not only put me on the CARE parcel list but also made up parcels of her own and they were life savers. Always a tin of ham, a tin of butter, lovely biscuits etc. We were much better off than many of our friends. Potatoes, root vegetables and any others we could get made up our diet. Oranges and bananas vanished altogether.

Wangy had left Yorkshire and had been made an Officer Commanding Troops at Sea, which meant that he commanded troop ships in convoys to the Mediterranean, North Africa, Italy, Sicily etc. Once he came home on leave in between ships. I had kept an egg, knowing he was due for leave. I kept it for three weeks. When he arrived I said, 'I've got an egg for you. How would you like it done?' He said that I must have it, not him. We argued about it until I said, 'All right, we'll share it.' So I fried it and turned it over and fried it on the other side. I also fried a big piece of bread, cut the egg in half and we thoroughly enjoyed it.

In the holidays Gary was a great little shopper. He would find some pies or a shop which had some sausages and bring them home to me in triumph. We all survived. I did get ill with my wretched chest but always got over it.

We lived in that flat for over two years, quite a record. I

obtained local war work of all kinds but I could never do anything special because of Gary's holidays. I got him a morning job at the Castle Theatre, sweeping the stage, collecting from local people, furniture and ornaments, pictures and anything else needed for the stage sets. A friend told me that Gary was a familiar sight going round with a handcart, asking people to lend their things, taking their names and addresses, giving receipts etc. He also helped the doorman, painted backcloths and picked up a lot of knowledge. By that time he was at Blundell's.

Farnham had some of the first rockets and doodle bugs, both very scary. We would watch a doodle bug coming over, wait to see if its engine was going to cut out and then dash downstairs to the cupboard under the stairs. A farmhouse one and a half miles away was flattened and everyone killed. But how lucky we three were. Wangy wrote to me once, 'I'll be lucky if I get through without being torpedoed. I see so many ships being blown up all around us.' They must have been a terrible sight and had a bad effect on him. Later on, when the war was over, he was dozing one afternoon, while I was washing up and calling out through the window over the sink to a passing friend, when Wangy appeared looking dazed and terrified. I asked him what was the matter and he said, 'I thought you were burning.' He also had very bad nightmares for some time.

I was quite alone in the flat in June 1944 and could not go to bed the night our troops went over for D Day. Troop carriers by the hundred flew over and I, knowing that Bernard was responsible for a lot of it, could only watch and pray for them.

After the war ended Margaret, who belonged to the British Red Cross, was taken away from Dumfries, fitted out with khaki uniform and told to report to London from where she was to fly to an unknown destination. I went to the airport to say goodbye to her and another woman from Scotland, a friend of hers. Never have I seen a more funny sight than Margaret, who is very short. She was in khaki trousers, gaiters, boots, hung all over with tin hat, tommie's cooker, knapsack etc., really funny. I said goodbye to them and in due course I had a postcard from Margaret just saying, 'We have arrived. I can't tell you where we are but it is a place very much in the public eye.' I could not think where it was. It turned out to be Belsen! These two girls were among the first lot of rescuers to go in and of course what they found was too ghastly for me to describe.

Margaret's job was always catering. Anything to do with food. She was taken to see an R.A.M.C. officer who said, 'Go to a certain ward where you will find eighty people dying or dead. Do what you can.' Margaret said 'I think there must be some mistake, Sir, I am not a nurse and I know nothing about it.' 'I don't give a damn what you are,' he said, 'you are English and a woman and you must do what you can.' All this was told to me by Margaret when she eventually came home. She told me that the emaciated people were indeed dying and many were dead, all suffering from tuberculosis, dysentery etc. etc. There was one thermometer and one bedpan. She was given two English soldiers and a lot of German women whom she could order to do anything she wanted. She made them put the people on a table and delouse them, the two soldiers standing guard with their rifles and fixed bayonets. I asked her how she stood what she did. She said that at intervals she would go to the lavatory, such as it was, and cry and be sick, but she did it. Margaret could do anything. Later a number of trained nurses arrived and were apparantly quite amazed at what they saw and how these two brave girls had coped.

II

Wangy came home on leave and said, 'Now I'm going to be retired where shall we live?' We decided on Devon, which we both knew well, so I went to visit some friends for three nights in a little place called Holcombe, outside Dawlish, and they advised me to come and stay in a very nice Guest House run by a Mrs. Brown, from which I could look for a house. I had the usual double bedroom, single bedroom for Gary and a very nice sitting room. Mrs. Brown was a dear and cooked very well. There were eggs and country food.

At last I met someone at a lunch party who asked what I was doing and when I said that I was house hunting she said, 'Oh, you had better come and live in "Larey's". I will tell Dr. Bertha Mules about you.' This lady, Miss Tritton, lived with Dr. Mules, who ran a big private mental home. 'Larey's', one of her houses, had been requisitioned by the W.R.N.S. but they were going and she wanted the house occupied at once in case any other organisation took it. I went to see her and the house, which was a lovely one with a wonderful view of the sea, on the Dawlish to Teignmouth road. Dr. Mules said that I could have it for a peppercorn rent but that she would not do it up, I must. So I took it over. The Wrens had had bunks which the Navy just ripped out. Everything was in a mess, but I wrote to Wangy, who was in the clearing up stage somewhere, the good news that we had a home. Somehow we got furniture; bits from Egypt and a few pieces from Pickford's that were left and we settled down.

Wangy was thin and not at all well, but the peace and the gardening did him good. Dr. Mules was a great help. She had four cars and not enough drivers, there was, I think, only one lady and her brother-in-law. She asked if Wangy would take charge of the cars, see that they were kept filled with petrol and, most important of all, drive her patients out. She called him her Transport Officer! It was just the job for him. He loved driving the patients and a nurse around. Dr. Mules owned a cottage up on Dartmoor and we used to pack up a picnic and go there on many an afternoon. The patients were not bad, just simple, and Wangy was specially good with them. In fact, on more than one occasion, he and I were sent out on quite long drives with two patients and no nurse, but we arrived home quite safely.

Gary, at this time, was just finishing at Blundell's and was ready for his National Service, or almost ready. He had an interval of three months to put in before his call up. Wangy said he must find something to do and he replied that he knew exactly what he wanted to do. He went over to Exmouth and got an interview with Bill Worsley, Director of the West of England Theatre Company and came home to me exclaiming that he had a job! He was on the stage management side and picked up a lot about acting. He and another boy, Charles Jarrett, were given digs with a very nice woman who fed them and looked after them like a mother. They left her house every morning with a packed lunch, had to report at the theatre, load up the van with stage properties and drive all round Devon to wherever there was a theatre; Totnes, Tiverton, Newton Abbot, even Teignmouth. On Teignmouth days he would warn us before and tell me what time they would be passing 'Larey's'. They hooted as they approached and I would hand out a cake.

After three months of that he was sent to Catterick in Yorkshire, to the Royal Signals. He chose that because he said that it had the largest Garrison Theatre in England. All the time his mind was set on the stage. It was hard work in the Signals but he did it all right and got his commission. Was I proud when he came home once during his two years in the uniform of an officer!

Then he went to Vancouver. This was at the request of a great aunt of his who, he found when he got there, had plans to put him into a banking business. He was furious and utterly refused.

Great Aunt was furious too. Gary then literally ran away, got on a Greyhound bus with very little more money than his fare and went to Toronto, where some cousins of his mother lived. We lost sight of him for a bit. When he wrote he was always in a different place doing odd jobs in theatres. I remember once hearing from somewhere in Louisiana, he had driven there in a van with a couple of people who put on a nightly puppet show. Such determination helped him through. He finally found his Mecca in Hollywood. Not to act, but to do all sorts of jobs, making money, always with his eyes on the stage. He became a very good photographer and did that for many years, living in a nice bungalow. I will tell you a lot more about him later.

After two and a half years at 'Larey's', Dr. Mules told us she wanted the house back. She had decided to fill it with patients and a couple of nurses. She gave us three months in which to find another house.

One day, a friend we had recently got to know, Sir Peter Hoare, rang me up saying, 'Mrs. Holderness, I hear you are looking for a house.' 'We are indeed,' I said, 'we have been all round here; Exmouth, Crediton and Dawlish and can't find anything we can afford.' 'Well,' he said, 'an old lady of ninety five, who has been in a house on my estate, has just died and I want to find good tenants. I am not interested in the rent, all I want is someone nice who will improve the garden and generally be an asset.' He told us to go and see his farm manager next day and arrange things with him. He did not sell any of his houses, only let them on twenty year leases.

Off we went by bus to Dawlish and a short walk up Luscombe Hill, where we met the manager. He took us up the hill a bit further and when we reached Oak Cottage Wangy dug me in the ribs and said, 'This is it.' It was an enchanting old house which had been two or three cottages years ago, now made into one. It had tall twisted chimneys and lattice windows with the old original lead panes. Mr. Lavis said that it was very run down. The old lady had done nothing to it for years, so he met us on several ideas. I wanted a Rayburn stove in the kitchen, for one, and he agreed to it.

Oak Cottage, Luscombe Hill, Dawlish.

We lost no time in moving in. It was the summer of 1949, a very dry summer I remember. It was pure paradise for us. We were right in the middle of woods, mostly beech trees. Sir Peter had a big shoot, so pheasants were all around us. I used to see as many as fourteen pheasants on the field in front of us. The keeper had coops of hens hatching out pheasant eggs and I loved to see the baby birds growing up.

We could not afford a car, but there was a bus which stopped a few hundred yards down the road. I was strong and a good walker and used to go to Dawlish once or twice a week to shop. Then, if there was too much to carry by bus, I would take a taxi. We had not many neighbours. There were only two more estate homes above us, but we made great friends with them and also with the Rayner family, who lived at the very top of the hill on Little Haldon at Ashcombe Tower.

Wangy used to boast that he never left the house and garden except to get his hair cut and to go to church on Sunday! He was was so happy learning to garden, working at it all day. He bought an Atco mowing machine at once, did away with a lot of fussy little flower beds and put them down to grass. We had a huge compost heap made by the estate carpenters, a two division affair. With loads of rotting beech leaves from the woods and our vegetable remains, we had as much of the most perfect compost as we could want.

We loved cats and had a succession, but alas they always got shot sooner or later by the keeper, so we were always renewing them! Wangy loved cats so much.

We soon had a very good vegetable garden going. Wangy grew every sort of vegetable, peas, beans, both string and broad, early potatoes, main crop potatoes, all salad stuff etc. We soon found it was quite impossible to grow for only two. Even though all the family visited us from time to time and I had huge dishes of all that was in season, there was still far more than we wanted. All our visitors went away laden, but still there was more. So at last we told everyone around us that if they liked to give us a weekly order we would supply them for just a few pence ('Just enough to pay for the seed,' Wangy said). That made it fun. We would find a basket and a list outside the back door and Wangy would wash his wares and bunch them up and have them ready for next day. It was a great success.

It was a proud day for us when we decided to enter our names for the local Agricultural Show, on Dawlish Lawn. We had to have a visit from the organizing secretary to make sure that we were not cheating! He gave us some good tips for presentation. How to smooth out runner beans to make them straight and a uniform length and how to twist the heads of shallots and 'size' them and place them in a box of sawdust. All this we did and nearly died of pride when Wangy got a First for his shallots and I got a Second for my Baby Royals (dahlias).

My mother died that first year. She had had a bad stroke three years before and though it did not in any way affect her mind it naturally weakened her as she was totally paralysed down her left side. There was no physiotherapy in those days, at least none in Moville. I went over to see her for three nights, which meant five nights away counting the journeys, then came home and Una replaced me. I received a telegram a few days later to say that Mother had died quite peacefully. I could not leave home and Wangy again, so sadly could not go to her funeral. Gary, who was at Catterick then, got leave and went.

We were so happy at Oak Cottage. It was so gloriously peaceful; right up in the woods with fields in front of us. We tamed lots of birds. We had a robin who would come into the kitchen, which opened on to the verandah, hop about and help himself to cake. Chaffinches also were very tame and used to tap with their beaks on my bedroom window if I was late in feeding them. We even taught the cats not to dash at them.

One day Wangy was in the wood shed chopping up logs for the fire when he heard a persistent mewing. He could see nothing for some time, then later he looked up to see a large black and white cat, one he had never seen before, running away. Still the mewing went on until he moved some logs and discovered two little black kittens. They were very wild and scared and would not let him touch them. So he came down to the house to tell me and I took a saucer of milk and put it outside the wood shed door. Nothing happened for some time but at last the two kittens came out and lapped up the milk. I refilled the saucer but put it nearer the house, until at last we got them right to the back door. We already had a house cat so decided that these must be outdoor cats and would never let them in. We made up a bed for them in an old trough in one of the sheds and they slept there. At Christmas, Gary sent them a Christmas card addressed to 'The Oak Cottage Twins' and I pinned it over their bed!

There came a day when Wangy, who had been upstairs for something, came to me saying, 'Go up to your bedroom and see something.' I went and there, on a little low armchair which I still have, were the two black kittens cuddled up together. They evidently thought it was time that they were acknowledged as house cats, so we allowed them in. I am sorry to say that the keeper shot one of them, but the other survived. We never saw the big black and white cat again, but it was quite obvious that she had had the kittens in our wood shed and would not leave them until she knew that they would be looked after. Poor, faithful mother.

12

Life went on in this peaceful way until Wangy started to have days when he felt terribly ill. This was in 1952. He would stay in bed but the doctor would come and find absolutely nothing wrong. The next day Wangy would have recovered. This happened three times in six months. Finally one night he pulled himself upstairs with great difficulty, saying he felt terribly ill. We had separate bedrooms, but I could not sleep for worry, so got up very early and went to his room to find him in a dreadful state. Suddenly he went into a rigor and started to shiver and shake. I rushed downstairs and made some very hot tea, seized an armful of blankets from the cupboard near the Rayburn and dashed back to give him the tea. He was very sick. It was obvious that he was seriously ill, so I rushed down to the telephone and woke up Dr. Lees demanding he should come. He did, took Wangy's temperature and blood pressure, then motioned me into the bathroom which was next door. He told me that his temperature was very high and his blood pressure very low. 'You must get a specialist here as soon as possible, as I do not know what is wrong,' he said, 'you will need a nurse but it is Whit Monday,' (it was June 2nd) 'and nurses are hard to get.' I replied that a near neighbour was a retired nurse and that I knew she would come and she did. Dr. Lees told me that a Dr. Daly would be there as soon as possible and, although it was his day off, he came.

I phoned Sir Peter at Dr. Daly's suggestion and asked for help. I told him that I had to have hospital equipment and I knew that the Matron of the Cottage Hospital would lend it to me. Sir Peter offered a car and one of his men, saying he could stay all day and do whatever we wanted. What a wonderful thing it is to have friends at such a time. Dr. Daly took charge, phoned Exeter for another nurse, took electrocardiographs. I did not know what was going on; all I knew was that help had come and I made tea and coffee at intervals.

Dr. Daly then told me that if Wangy lived through the night he must go into hospital and an ambulance would come for him. He did survive the night although at 5 a.m. the nurse called me as he thought he was dying and wanted to speak to me. We went up in an ambulance during the morning and Wangy never saw his beloved Oak Cottage again. We both gained a friend in Dr. Daly, who is still the best and most loved friend I have. It took him three days to discover what was the cause of this illness. It was a very rare organism called B. Pyocyanea which has this peculiarity, that once the organism gets into the blood stream it takes six months to hatch; hence the three days of illness at intervals until the fateful day on which it hatched.

After pathological investigations it was found that Wangy had septicaemia due to this organism, which had spread to the heart, urine and right shoulder. The latter was hurting him so dreadfully that Mr. Durbin, the surgeon, opened it up and released the pus which had formed there. The formation of pus is typical of B. Pyocyanea. There were no antibiotics at that time to which this would respond, but in the end a new drug was obtained from the Wellcombe Institute and with this the infection was quickly controlled.

By 23rd June the actual disease was probably cured, but the heart performance was still very uncertain and Dr. Daly said, 'As I have no previous experience of this condition and am very young (thirty nine), I am going to arrange transfer to the London Hospital, to be under Sir Horace Evans, who taught me all I know.'

We left the Royal Devon and Exeter Hospital by ambulance which took us to St. David's Station to catch the 7.30 a.m. train for London. Sister Butler of Dean Clarke Ward accompanied us. Everything was so wonderfully arranged. Wangy was on a stretcher, which was slid straight into a carriage and put on a seat, and Sister had a case of necessary nursing things. One of us was with him all the time. When she went off to the restaurant car for coffee, I remained, then I went and she stayed. He stood the journey very well and we were met by another ambulance and driven quickly to the London Hospital and Gloucester Ward. Dr. Daly's orders to me had been to go with him and stay as near as possible as I was very necessary to him. Up to then I had been staying in Exeter, first at the Royal Clarence Hotel, until I could no longer afford it, then with a kind friend, Dr. Irene Ward.

When we arrived at the hospital, I said goodbye to Sister Butler, saw Wangy settled in Gloucester Ward, then went to see the Lady Almoner. I told her that Dr. Daly had told me to come and ask her if she could find somewhere for me to stay, as near to the hospital as possible. She said that it was impossible to find anywhere nice, but there was a public house, which had a restaurant and a grill room and several bedrooms which they let, at Aldgate, about a mile and a half down the Whitechapel Road. The almoner said that it was not a nice place and probably I would not like it, but the owners were straight and I would be safe. So I went along at once, saw the owner and took a bedroom. There I stayed for two months.

The bed had clean sheets and blankets and they and the towel were changed once a week, but the carpet was so stained that I never dared to put a bare foot on it and always put my slippers on first. The bath was dreadful, so I went to Woolworth's and bought Vim and a cloth and washed it every time I got in. The lavatory was dreadful also, always awash by night time! But, and a big but, the owners were kindly and sympathetic. They soon got to know of my trouble for the sister of the ward had to send for me many times, often during a meal. I had a table facing the door and would look up to see the very nice hall porter beckoning to me. 'Sister wants you,' he would say. I remember during the two months I was there I was sent for eleven times at night.

Wangy had recurring attacks of cardiac asthma. Always they thought that he could not pull through but due to their wonderful care and his fighting spirit he did. He was usually drowsy with sedatives when I arrived and just very glad to see me. He did not ask questions. Only once, when they had put me to finish the night on a bed in the next ward and I appeared at six o'clock to give him his early tea, did he ask why I was so early. 'Oh,' I said, 'it's such a glorious morning that I thought I would get up and have a walk.'

Every night that I was sent for and after I had seen Wangy, I went down to the Blood Donors waiting room where relatives of patients were allowed to sleep for the rest of the night. It was wonderfully organised with bunk beds and blankets and at about half past five a large tray with a huge pot of tea and a big plate of bread and butter was brought in. Sometimes there were five or six of us, sometimes only one and once, when I was alone, I had a creepy shock when a white coated man, a young doctor, came in, opened the 'frig.' and took out a bottle of blood! Two or three nights running there was a man there whose wife was dying. He told me all about himself; he was a driver of a lorry which took vegetables to Covent Garden and he offered to take me one morning, but he never appeared again, his wife died.

I used to feed Wangy a lot, Sister said that it helped them. I asked her one day if the other patients did not mind me being there all day, as visiting hours were strict. 'No, my dear,' Sister said, 'all these men have seen the Colonel in his attacks and they realise that you must be there.' They were all such nice men. Wangy told me that he learned a great deal about human nature in that ward.

Now I will tell you a really funny story. A great many of his fellow patients were Jews and Wangy took a lot of interest in them. There was a little Jewish tailor called Emmanuel in a bed the other side of the ward, but opposite to Wangy. He, Emmanuel, suffered from some kidney complaint and had to have his output measured. To save the nurses trouble and to give himself something to do he used to take his bottle down to the sluice room, measure the contents and come back to put the amount on the chart which hung at the foot of his bed. One day when Matron came in, Emmanuel was stooping down writing up his chart. Matron stood there with her arms folded and said, 'May I ask you what you are doing?' Emmanuel whipped round and said, 'Measuring up my exports Matron, vital for the nation.' Wangy said that he nearly burst himself and Matron put her hand over her mouth and left the ward as quickly as she could.

I also saw a lot of Jewish life in Whitechapel Road. I shall never forget the smell of stewed eels, I can smell it still. Then there was a woman who went up and down the road every day crying, 'Buy my argels, dear.' I never found out what argels were, but think they were some sort of rolls. She and I got to know each other.

To return to my life at the pub, which was called the Three Nuns, as well as the nice hotel porter there was a waitress called Mabel who took me under her wing and always waited on me. Every morning she would put her hand in her pocket and bring me out two or three lumps of sugar. 'There you are dear,' she would say, 'I've saved these for you.' They would be all mixed up with cigarette ends and bits of fluff, but they tasted very sweet to me.

There was a dear little church almost next door to the Three Nuns and I went there every day before going to the hospital. I got to know the Rector, who took the early service. One day he asked me if I would like to see 'their great treasure'. I said, 'Yes please,' and he took me into the vestry, unlocked a cupboard and took out something in a square glass case. 'This,' he said, 'is the mummified head of the Duke of Somerset, brother of Lady Jane Grey. He was beheaded in the Tower, quite close, and three nuns who were watching came forward and gathered up the head and pressed all round it a quantity of sawdust from the oak block on which he had lain his head.' Apparently oak sawdust is very air proof and, of course, it soaked up the blood and then preserved it. The macabre thing was that at the back of the neck you can see a dent where the executioner missed his first blow and then the whole cut off neck is exposed. The mummy is perfect, just a small, shrunken head. I do not think many people know about it, so I felt very privileged to see it.

When Wangy was getting better he was able to get up and dress and sit out on a balcony talking to other patients. This gave me an opportunity to go out too. Our dear American friend Helen Benson, the one who used to send us food parcels during the war, came over especially to see us and stayed at the Ritz, where Wangy and I had often stayed with her. There is a wonderful bus, I forget its number, which runs from Whitechapel to the top of Piccadilly. The bus stop was opposite the Three Nuns, so all I had to do was to step on it and in half an hour or so be transported from a slum to one of the biggest hotels in London where I was fêted and fed royally. My clothes were pretty awful, I had only what I had snatched away in a hurry, but I went to Swan and Edgar one day and got a nice dress and that, with a pair of white gloves, saw me through. Helen used to visit Wangy a lot and take him luxury food such as a little cold roast snipe or half a small chicken, whatever caught her eye at Fortnum and Mason.

Another day I went to tea with Lady Rayner who had come up to London for a few days. I must not forget to mention that Brigadier Sir Ralph and Lady Rayner were true friends all through Wangy's illness, always ready with help, offers of transport etc. They remained lifelong friends, I have been to the weddings of all their four children and have had many a good time at their house.

I always had my lunch, while I was in Whitechapel, at a little pub across the road from the hospital, I think it was called the Bunch of Grapes. I got a good big plateful of chicken stew and vegetables for one shilling and threepence. A good many of the doctors from 'The London' went there and before I left I took the young doctor who was the house physician to Dr. Balme and who had looked after Wangy devotedly, to lunch there. I gave him more than one drink before his lunch and talked a lot with him. He told me that 'The Colonel' was the bravest man he had ever met and he was sure he would never have another patient like him. What they all loved about him was the way he joked. He told me that one day he drew off a great deal of liquid from Wangy's lung and said, 'There you are Colonel, there's a pint of good golden liquid for you.' To which Wangy replied, 'Well it's not whisky, so it's not much good to me.'

I paid six pounds a week for my room at the Three Nuns, that was in 1952. I suppose it included breakfast, which was as good a meal as you could get in those days, when food was still not very lavish. As I say, I lunched at the Bunch of Grapes and I had dinner in the hotel, but not in the grill room, which was a very good and quite well known one. The clientèle of the Three Nuns was entirely commercial travellers so no one was there at the weekends.

13

At long last, after two months, Wangy was pronounced fit to return to the Royal Devon and Exeter Hospital. We left, as we had arrived, by ambulance to the station with a junior nurse to look after him. The train journey was quite easy and once arrived he was under Dr. Daly's care again. I went back to Oak Cottage to pack up and leave, although I did not yet know what we were going to do. All I knew was Sir Horace Evans's ultimatum; 'No more stairs. No more gardening.' It was a very difficult thing for me to have to see Sir Peter and ask him to let me break the twenty year lease of the house, but he agreed most nobly.

It was lovely getting back to the country though and I was so happy to see my friends and enjoy the garden. I cannot remember what had happened to the cats! Poor little things, perhaps they had been shot. I got my clothes straight, sorted and packed up the house, said goodbyes and made trips to Exeter by bus to see Wangy, who got steadily stronger. Finally Dr. Daly told us that he thought a good place where Wangy could really recuperate was a hotel at Chagford. It was all built on bungalow lines so there would be no stairs and there was a lovely garden and glorious views of Dartmoor. We booked a big double bedroom there and drove up. We could not have found a nicer place. It was called Great Tree Hotel and it is still there. The garden was a large one with a greenhouse and a real Devonian gardener. This was a joy to Wangy who spent a lot of time out there talking to him. Also in the hotel we made friends with a couple, a little older than we were, who lived there permanently. Wangy and the husband spent hours together watching cricket on television.

Dr. Daly had handed us over to a very nice doctor who also

Wangy and the gardener at Chagford. 1952

became a real friend and kept a keen eye on Wangy. We had put all the contents of Oak Cottage into store in Dawlish, so only had personal possessions with us. It was a nice, lazy interlude and I really enjoyed it, although I could see our money slipping away! Wangy was able to walk about the garden and gradually got stronger. All we had to do was to 'wait on' Dr. Daly, as the Irish would say.

Before we went to Chagford, Dr. Daly had asked me what I had in mind for the future, where I wanted to live and in what. I had said, 'Exeter please, so as to be near you, and the cheapest ground floor flat possible.' Suddenly one morning in the spring, I remember it so well, I was told that I was wanted on the telephone. It was Dr. Daly to tell me that a colleague of his, a general practitioner in Exeter, was leaving a ground floor flat as he was building a house up at the top of Pennsylvania. If I was interested, here was the name of the landlord and I had better get in and see him as soon as possible. I rushed off at once and had a preliminary talk, but said that Wangy must come and see things for himself. I think we must have hired a car. I know this nice landlord came to see us at the Imperial Hotel, which we chose as it had a good comfortable lounge where the two men could sit and discuss business. Also, of course, I had to see the flat.

Dr. Merrick, the doctor who had already moved out, had only had it temporarily I believe and I do not think that he and his wife were any more enamoured of it than I was. It was a dark little place and very cold, but at least it had no stairs. It had no garden itself but it was in a very nice road with other good big gardens and, best of all, Dr. Merrick became our friend as well as our doctor.

The flat was one of a little block built on a bombed site. West Avenue had had a stick of incendiary bombs down it and these modern atrocities were built on the bare places. We ordered our furniture to come up and we moved in. We soon made many friends in the road and Wangy really progressed in health for a bit. He was never able to do much, but he could enjoy seeing people and we would hire a car to take us to the Cathedral and sometimes he even walked into town. Nevertheless it was only a case of encouraging ourselves that he was really getting better. We knew that he could not live long and it was bitter to see his frustration. All I could do was to love and care for him. Such good friends we had. All through our married life our friends meant so much to us and what we would have done while at West Avenue without Dr. Merrick always at hand and Dr. Daly always in the background, I do not know.

I do not know where Gary was all this time but he was acting somewhere. He had come back to England, I expect because of me, and was working in various repertory companies. He would turn up for a day sometimes to see us, then disappear again. One visitor who gave Wangy very much pleasure was the then Dean of Exeter, Alec Wallace. He had been in India in his youth and knew the North West Frontier, where Wangy had served for so long. Many a time he would come up to see us and I would leave the two men to yarn happily away.

But all the time we knew it could not last and four years later he had a colossal heart attack one night. Dr. Merrick came, it was eleven o'clock at night, he called Dr. Daly who came at once and ordered a nurse in. All such familiar history. No one could have imagined anyone could live through that night. Dr. Daly put his hand on my arm, I remember, and said, 'Well my dear, this is what we have been waiting for, for four years.' But he did not die that night. We had two nurses, one day and one night and they kept him as comfortable as they could. Finally, and mercifully, the end came suddenly and unexpectedly, an embolism on a Sunday morning. The night nurse had just left and I was going to be the day nurse, as there were no nurses on Sundays. I had left him for a moment, heard him and rushed in to find that he had died.

I sent a car to our dear day nurse's home to ask her to come, knowing she would and she did at once for she was so fond of him. Dr. Daly and his wife came, the Dean came and a nice friend who lived near came at Dr. Merrick's direction, to be with me all day until Gary arrived.

I had quite a job to find him as I did not know where he was. I phoned a friend of his who told me he was acting in Amersham.

I soon got hold of him and he said he would arrive by the evening.

We buried Wangy at Alphington, a real country cemetery, under a tree which was full of birds. Brian came from London with many messages from Bernard, who was unable to get away. He had ordered Brian to find out how I was situated, if I knew how to get my army pension, all that sort of thing, and a day or two later I got a nice present of money from him. Wangy died on December 16th and was buried three days later so Christmas was only a week away. The Dean said that I was to spend it at the Deanery, which I gladly did.

Then life was one big bustle and hustle for Helen Benson wrote and said there were to be no objections, I was to go to America and stay with her, all expenses paid. In those days you could take only a very small amount of cash out of England, ten pounds, can you imagine it?

I stayed on for a bit to get my breath as it were, to sort out my money affairs, say goodbye to West Avenue and get some clothes made to take away. Gary appeared again, took charge of my travel arrangements and took me to London to get my passport. I was to go out by boat to join Helen in Miami, where she usually spent the winter as she had a house there. The boat sailed from Liverpool so I went to Wallasey to stay with Colin and Margaret. That boat, I have forgotten the line or the name, took an extraordinary route from Liverpool to Santander and somewhere else in Spain, then out across the Atlantic to Bermuda. We had to stop there for twenty four hours because something was wrong in the engine room. Nobody minded after an English winter. It was now February and wonderful to be in such a paradise of beauty.

I was at a table of people much younger than I and they all wanted to go ashore. The Company put on a launch for us as we were going to have a long day with nothing to do. One problem these young people pointed out was that none of us had any money so how were we going to feed ourselves and could I think of anything? I went to the Head Steward and asked, as he had not got to feed us on board, whether he would pack up a big lunch box. He agreed, and so we set off for the shore and began to look at Bermuda. We wanted to go and have our lunch on a real coral beach, so we hired a taxi, first bargaining with the driver to take us for as little as possible, and we all solemnly contributed part of the fare. It was all very light hearted and delightful and we caught the launch back in good time for dinner.

Next day we arrived at Nassau which was our destination. We got in quite early, but I had to wait some hours before I could get a plane for Miami. I was quite happy wandering around Nassau, which is a fascinating place, but I cannot remember what I had to eat. Going on the plane gave me a thrill as I had never flown before and I found it most exciting to come down over Miami with all the lights beginning to go up and thousands of car lights making it look like a rippling necklace. Helen and her faithful maid/companion Henny were waiting to meet me and took me at once to a lovely restaurant for dinner.

Then to the house, a very big bungalow, with a large garden. It was full of pineapples and other exotic fruits growing as we would grow cabbages. There were lots of quails who say, 'Bob white, bob white,' all the time and in fact they are known locally as 'Bob Whites'. I was shown all the sights, the Everglades and Key West and the amazing beaches. We went to Palm Beach, a very luxurious, pretty town. Everything was so new to me. We were there for two months, then we drove up to Princeton, which was Helen's real home.

It was a most interesting drive all through the southern states, up through North and South Carolina, Maryland and into New Jersey. We spent each night in a motel, until at last we reached Princeton and the beautiful house in which I was to make my home for the next few months. Never had I had such a luxurious bedroom and bathroom as those which were mine. American hospitality is out of this world. The bathroom was stocked with every sort of cosmetic one could want. The bedroom had a beautiful divan to rest on, a big writing desk stocked with all sizes of writing paper, air mail letters, stamps, all renewed as I used them. I found it quite bewildering.

We settled down to Helen's routine. She loved racing, so every week we went to one of the big racecourses. I am not interested in the sport so found it a bit boring but most days we would drive out round the country and that I did love. We drove all over the states of Pennsylvania and New Jersey. One day we had a long drive to Detroit where Helen had a horse at stud.

Then, every Wednesday, we would make an early start for New York. Helen told me that she went up for massage, hair appointments and I don't know what else, but I was to be on my own all day, free to explore New York, meeting her and Henny again at the corner of East 49th Street and Madison Avenue, at a garage there. I gasped at the thought of being alone in New York, how would I find my way? 'Quite easy,' said Helen, 'all the streets go across avenues and Central Avenue is the one where you will start.' She was right. It was easy and I began to look forward to Wednesdays.

I started with the shops, of course, all the big, well known ones. Helen gave me a small amount of money each time with which to get my lunch and pay a bus fare. I sat on stools in little restaurants to have a light lunch and often people hearing my English accent would speak to me. I always made for the Museum of Modern Art and spent two or three hours there for I am very fond of pictures. I decided that I would try and teach myself the difference between the Impressionists, whom I love. How to tell a Manet, a Monet, a Degas or a Van Gogh (he was easy). I also looked at the beautiful ceramics and antique jewellery.

I began to get restive after a few months of all this. I am an independant person and did not like being 'kept', so I said, 'Please may I go home?' Helen replied that I must see Niagara before I left, so we drove up there all through New York State, past Lake Placid and clear up to the Canadian lakes of a thousand islands. Niagara Falls, of course, were stupendous.

14

People may wonder how I spent my meagre sterling allowance in America. I hoarded it like a miser. I doled out a certain sum, just enough to put in the collection bag at church on Sundays and I was determined to give Helen a little present before I left, but could not think what to get as she had everything. One day, when discussing it with Henny, her maid, Henny suddenly said, 'I know, Mrs.Benson is always saying she really must get some dog wood trees to plant by the swimming pool, but she never does.' So I rang up a nursery garden and ordered half a dozen dog wood trees to be delivered the day after I left. Dog wood is a lovely tree with a pretty white blossom and the leaves turn a brilliant red gold in the autumn.

When I decided to come home I did not know where to go. In the end I wrote to the Rector of Alphington and asked if I could be a paying guest until I found a flat. I offered to pay five pounds a week and to do all the cooking. When this was fixed, my passage was booked for Liverpool, Helen and Henny saw me off and the voyage was quite uneventful.

The exciting part was my arrival. I was so thrilled to be back in England, I was like a child, hanging out of the train window, looking at the fields and the hedges, the ponies and the sheep. When I got out of the taxi on arrival at Alphington Rectory, Ruth, the Rector's wife, was in the hall in Civil Defence uniform. She held out her arms and said, 'Welcome! Over to you, I'm just off to Bristol for the night. Will you cook supper for yourself and William and breakfast tomorrow and take charge generally until I come back?' Just like that! I was certainly thrown at once into the sort of job I wanted. I found a big bedroom ready for me, unpacked and settled down.

At that time England was Civil Defence mad. Everyone was learning how to protect their homes from gas attacks amid fears of another war. There were evening lectures on First Aid, how to seal tins of food and cupboards and windows and how to build ovens out of doors in case houses were bombed. Oh! Those ovens, they were a job I shall never forget. We collected bricks and built hollow squares with them with a sort of trivet inside. It was too hard a job for me.

I was made to join the Women's Voluntary Service, the W.V.S. as it was called then although now it has 'Royal' in it of course. I got my uniform after a bit and was given various things to do. Lady Reading came to Exeter to speak and there was a lunch afterwards which we had to provide. My first assignment was to make fruit salad for one hundred people. It sounded a large order but I had a friend who pointed out to me that it only meant working out how much to make for ten and then multiplying it by ten.

I also found work in Exeter, only a short bus ride away. I went to see the Matron of the Royal Devon and Exeter Hospital in Southernhay and asked if I could be of use in any of the wards. Matron said that I would be very useful in the children's ward in the afternoons, which, of course, was just what I wanted. I got the teas, sat with children who were coming round from operations, read to those who were convalescing, gave babies their bottles and things like that. I loved it all. Then back to the Rectory by six o'clock to cook supper and spend the evening listening to the wireless and talking to William and Ruth.

Several of my family came to see me while I was there. My brother Donald came over from Vancouver, also Colin and Margaret, home on holiday from the parish they had gone to in South Africa. Then the inevitable happened. I was doing too much, the Rectory was bitterly cold and once again I went down with pneumonia.

After I recovered from that I did go away for six weeks to Bournemouth. I stayed in an hotel there with my cousin, Hilda Montgomery, who asked me to go and keep her company.

Finally Dr. Daly stepped in, saying that the Rectory was far too cold and, having been there for eighteen months, I must seriously look for something else.

So he got busy for me and while I was in Bournemouth I had a letter from him saying that he had found a little flat. It was in a block that had just been built by a patient of his, Mr. Davey, in St. Leonard's Road, and it was just the place for me as it was small, but compact and very sunny. He had been to so much trouble for me, going to see it twice and taking his wife the second time to obtain a woman's approval. The only thing was that I must make up my mind at once. The flats, eight in all, were being snapped up but Mr. Davey would keep this one for me for forty eight hours. I telephoned the Deanery and asked Mrs. Wallace if she would put me up, got on a coach, made an appointment to see Mr. Davey, liked the flat and took it. As it was at the back of the block it was very quiet and as it faced due South sunshine could pour in all day.

I returned to the Rectory and broke the news to Ruth that she would lose her cook. She actually cried, poor Ruth! William understood and said that I was now ready to stand on my own feet again, and he was glad.

I got my furniture out of store, bought material and had curtains made and a cover for a divan which I had instead of a bed. I only had one room, a kitchen, a tiny dressing room and a very nice bathroom. I wanted the one living room to look like one, and not like a bedroom; the result was good, it did. The kitchen window looked out on to Wonford Road, so I saw people and cars passing and I was up one flight of stairs with three windows in the living room, which got the sun all day. As it was such a small flat I could, of course, choose just the best bits of my furniture, though the smallest. I think that it looked quite nice by the time I had it all straight and I settled down to many happy years there. No more moves for thirteen years! I owed it all to Dr. Daly who came to my rescue in every time of difficulty.

I carried on with my afternoons at the Hospital and I did various things with the W.V.S. I helped with 'Meals on Wheels' where, as I was not a driver, I was the driver's mate and took the meals in to the old people which was interesting. Later on I added the Hospital Library, where I worked at night taking a big trolley load of books round the wards. Finally a great friend from Oak Cottage days, Lady Rayner (Betty) came to see me one day and told me that she had a job which she hoped I would do. It was to be what she called a liaison officer at 'The Lodge' in Spicer Road, a new home just opened by the Distressed Gentlefolk's Aid Association, known as the D.G.A.A. She was the President and Chairman of the Committee. They had only just started and she thought it was a job which I could do, as I liked people. I was to be the confidante of both the residents and the Matron; just to listen to everyone and to help where I could. I was voted onto the Committee and remained on it for twenty years.

After a year or two, I was appointed the Representative of 'The Lodge'. I had to go to London on the first Monday of the month, to Vicarage Gate House in Kensington, that being the Headquarters of the Association. There I had to give a report on the activities, and perhaps difficulties, at 'The Lodge', ask for guidance and hear similar reports from representatives of the other homes.

Betty Rayner certainly gave me a very interesting occupation. I was a constant visitor and used to have to do some funny things. One evening Matron rang me up and asked me if I would go round at once and help her with a male resident who had been out and returned so drunk that they could not get him upstairs! I phoned a man friend of mine, who arrived and got him up to his room safely. That was just one of the teething troubles of a new Home. It all settled down very soon, rules were made and kept, and now it is a very thriving, successful and much loved Home for elderly gentlefolk, with two nursing wings and a big staff. I retired from the Committee as a Founder Member twenty years after but long before that I had handed over being 'The Lodge's' representative.

The highlight of those first Mondays was that they gave me a chance to see Brian and his dear wife Bunty, who lived in Chelsea. I went straight to their house for an early lunch, then Bunty would drive me to Vicarage Gate in time for the meeting at half past two and I would go home on the half past four train. Brian and Bunty once came to Exeter to see me and they loved my little flat.

I made several trips abroad during this time, always in the winter so as to get away from the cold. One year I went to Rhodesia for three months to stay with Holderness cousins. I had the most wonderful time with them. I stayed on a tobacco farm with John Holderness. I made my headquarters with his mother, Connie, and from her house I visited all the rest of the family, and I saw quite a lot of the country.

I went on a memorable day trip to the Victoria Falls, so beautiful it is impossible for me to try and describe them. There were herds of elephants trampling down the undergrowth and monkeys leaping about in the trees, and everywhere the noise of the Falls, with the beautiful spray, which meant there was always a rainbow. It was a long day for I had left Salisbury on the 7 a.m. plane and I did not get home to Connie until dinner time at 7.30 p.m. I had gone alone as all the family were busy. They were a most charming family and I made great friends with them all. They tried to persuade me to say that I would leave England and live out there but nothing would make me. I love England and Ireland too much, but those winters away from the cold at home did me a lot of good.

Gary, by that time, was in America and twice I went to Los Angeles to stay with him and keep house for him for three months. He took me about and showed me all around California. We had three memorable days in San Francisco, which to me is the most fascinating city in the world. We drove up by the coast road, going through Santa Barbara, Carmel and Monterey and I saw oil rigs standing out in the sea for the first time. They were such strange looking things.

Another time he took me for just a short, three day visit to Mexico, to a little shrimping village on the Gulf of California. It was called San Felipe and Gary said that it was his favourite place, so he was very glad when he found that I liked it also. It was just a simple little fishing village with the boats going out in the morning and returning in the evening with their catch. We could only manage a few words of Spanish and the managers of the little hotel where we stayed could only speak a little English, but we managed.

The long road out to San Felipe was through a wild desert which seemed to go on for ever. We never passed or saw another car and every now and then we passed black crosses by the road-side which Gary said marked the places where there had been a fatal accident. In the middle of the desert I was cheered by suddenly seeing trees and what looked like a lake. 'Oh look,' I said, 'there's water ahead. We are coming to an oasis.' Gary laughed and said, 'That's not an oasis, it's a mirage!' The first I had ever seen, for funnily enough I never saw one in Egypt.

Another time on one of my visits to California my brother Donald wrote and asked me if I would go and stay with him and a friend of his who were going to be in Palm Springs for their annual holiday. Donald told me to go there by Greyhound bus so off I went through a lot of desert and some rather dull towns, and then to Palm Springs, which is really a big oasis full of lovely private homes and hotels. We were in an hotel. My little bedroom was on the edge of the swimming pool, with Donald close by. His room had a little kitchenette, in which he made breakfast for the three of us. One evening we had dinner with a client of his, who lived in a beautiful bungalow surrounded by a lovely garden full of orange and lime trees. Our host said, 'Would you like a gin and lime?' When I said, 'Yes please,' he went into the garden, picked some limes and squeezed them into the gin and ice. Quite delicious. Again I was in California for three months altogether.

15

Those visits accounted for three years. Busy years they were and very happy. I soon found that a lone widow gets asked to do all sorts of odd jobs. One friend who could not cook, and knew I loved cooking, frequently asked me to make cold dishes for her lunch parties. Her favourite was 'A large asparagus mousse, enough for eight people please.' Of course she paid for all the materials and she would come and collect it an hour before lunch.

Another time I was let in for a job I did not like. Mrs. Hall, the wife of one of the Canons of the Cathedral, came to see me and said that she had a great favour to ask. Would I go and be the temporary Warden for a month at 'Tranquility', which is a Holiday Home for clergy and their wives in Torquay. It had been founded by an elderly benefactress and was so heavily subsidised that the visitors only paid three pounds per week. I was appalled and said that I could not possibly do it, but Mrs. Hall said, 'Please you must. The Warden is going away for her annual holiday and the Committee cannot find a replacement.' She had suggested me as she knew I liked dealing with people. She said that she would drive me down to inspect it and have a talk with the Warden, and that is what we did. Really what I had to do was to be a hostess; meet the visitors when they arrived, tell them the rules and times of meals etc. and, this was what I dreaded, collect money from the bank each week and pay the wages to the staff. I am hopeless with money and the thought of those little bags full of various coins, halfcrowns, sixpences etc. terrified me, but they succeeded in talking me into it and I went.

It was quite fun in some ways. I used to go to the front door to find a tired couple, I would ask them if the parson liked to be called 'Father' or 'Mister' (my idea!) and take them to their room. It was fun to see the look of thrilled surprise when I told them that tea would be brought to them in the morning at eight o'clock and it was heartening to see them relax and lose their look of weariness. They tended to sit in the sun on the terrace overlooking the harbour for several days, then as they got rested they took to going down into Torquay and walking about on the sea front, looking at the shops and so on. In the afternoons I would preside at a teatable in the drawing room. Rules were strict, one was NO SMOKING in the drawing room. Anyone who wanted to smoke had to do so in the smoking room. Many of the wives smoked and naturally wanted to do so with their husbands after tea, but I pointed out the Charter which hung up, framed, for all of them to see! It was a funny life. When I left I vowed I would never do it again, but Mrs. Hall persuaded me to do it once more. Then I struck and firmly refused to do it a third time and they managed to find someone else.

All this time I was in constant touch with my family. As I have already said, I saw Brian and Bunty every month and the Canadian contingent came over every few years when we would all foregather. Colin, alas, died two years after Wangy, so Margaret was a widow like me. She lived in Belfast for a bit then made her home in Kirkcudbright; she is still there and we exchange visits. Bernard, when he retired as a Field Marshal, lived at 'The Mill' in a little village called Binsted, near Alton in Hampshire. He made a lovely, very unusual home in the old mill and we were often bidden to a lunch or to a party. He liked us just to talk 'family' and Brian used to lead him on to tell stories of the past. I can hear Brian now saying, 'Come on Bernard, tell us the story of the cow,' and Bernard would begin, then laugh so much that he had to cover his face with a handkerchief.

After having had three Christmases away in other, warmer, countries I took to giving myself the treat of spending the three or four days of Christmas at the Royal Clarence Hotel in Exeter. That saved me the bother of a lot of cooking and no one had to worry about me, but best of all I was right next to my beloved Cathedral and could go to all the services I wanted to. I imagined that this happy life would go on for ever, but somehow I began to feel a bit lonely, I seemed to have no real object in life, perhaps because I had looked after so many people and now there was no one.

It was the summer of 1970. There was a big Flower Festival in the Cathedral, a three day event, so naturallly every member of the congregation was called upon to help. My job was to sit at a table in one of the aisles with a big silver tray in front of me, ready for contributions of money. One evening Sir Godwin Michelmore came in from his office in Cathedral Yard at about half past six. I only knew him slightly, I had met him a few times and both of us were on the Council of the Friends of the Cathedral. I knew he was a widower, living alone in St. Leonard's Road. I also knew he was a very keen gardener, invariably on his knees in his front garden, weeding or planting. I would stop and say good morning and perhaps comment on his roses.

When he came up to my table that evening he stopped and put a fiver in my tray which pleased me, as a fiver then meant more than it does now. He then asked me what the Festival was about and whether it was worth looking at. 'Indeed it is,' I said, so he asked me if I would show him around and explain it. I replied that I would be delighted to, if he would wait about five minutes, when my time of duty would be up. Then off we went, with me pointing out all the wonderful displays. When we had made the grand tour he asked how I was going home. I said that I walked, to which he replied, 'Don't do that. Let me give you a lift. I am going to have a car, as I always do, from Underhill's just down the road.' We set off in the car and on the way he asked me to come in and have a drink. That started off a very nice acquaintanceship and for the next few months I saw quite a lot of him and liked him very much.

One thing I tried to do for him was to get him a new housekeeper, as his previous one had sadly had to leave him. Although I wrote to several agencies all over the country I failed to find anyone. No one noticed it, but I went to his house, number ten, more and more and he sometimes came to see me. I realised that I had lost my heart to him, a thing I had never expected to do again.

Finally, one evening in November, he asked me to come and have a drink and stay on to supper, which I would cook! We arranged it all very nicely and the inevitable happened. He asked me to marry him. I need hardly say that he actually asked me in the kitchen, so that afterwards I always said that he only asked me in order to get a cook and a housekeeper! It was a wonderfully happy evening and he saw me home, both of us walking on air. He explained that we could not tell anyone our news for a week as Jim and June, his son and daughter-in-law, were abroad and we must wait for their return. This meant, of course, that I could not tell either of my brothers, so for a whole week we hugged our news to ourselves, fell more and more in love and got to know each other better and better.

At last the evening came when Godwin said that Jim and June would be coming in for a drink to tell him about their holiday and I must be there. I was horrified and said that I could not possibly be present, as they might be dreadfully upset and I would not be able to bear to see their faces. Godwin said, 'All right, I will tell them, then phone you and you must come at once.' The phone rang at last. Godwin said, 'Darling, they're here and it's all right. Come quickly.' I fairly ran down the road, rushed into the house and literally into their arms, both of them hugging and kissing me. Oh! What a relief! Then there was Jim with a note pad and pen scribbling something and when I asked him what he was doing he said, 'Writing your engagement notice, of course. Give me the proper names of your family, your late husband etc. and now you can tell your brothers.' I rang up Bernard and Brian and told them. They were both thrilled. I told them that Godwin was a Major General in the Territorial Army, with every sort of letter after his name, and that as this was a Sunday the notice could not be in the papers until Tuesday. We had one more day of secrecy until the notice appeared, then life was one mad rush. Godwin said, 'Marry me before Christmas,' to which I replied, 'Ridiculous, I could not possibly be ready before the New Year.'

We got engaged on November 26th and we phoned Bishop Westall to ask him to marry us. He was so sweet. I asked him if we could be married on January 2nd and he at once said 'Yes'. 'But Wilfred,' I said, 'you haven't looked at your diary.' 'Blast my diary!' said the Bishop.

Bernard said he would come to Exeter and give me away and he was so pleased and excited that he sent me a cheque for one hundred pounds, both the envelope and the cheque made out to Mrs. Winsome Montgomery! I suppose, in his excitement, I was just his young sister again. I wondered how I would cash that cheque, but Godwin took me to see my bank manager and asked him how he could get round such a thing. 'Don't worry,' said Mr. Crews, 'I know the manager of Lloyds Bank in Farnham and I will phone him and he will put it through at once.' He did, and of course I never told Bernard, but I still have that envelope which is a very precious possession.

16

We fixed Saturday, January 2nd 1971 for our wedding day and how we got everything settled in time I shall never know. There was so much to be done. I had to give notice to give up my little flat, book a removal man to empty it a week or two after our wedding and bring everything to No. 10, I had to buy my wedding outfit, and, when I did, all the sales people had seen the notices in the 'Express and Echo' and other papers and knew I was marrying Sir Godwin Michelmore. They also knew that I was Monty's sister and every one of them seemed to have had a husband or son in the Eighth Army and said they would turn out in force, which they did. Jim and June were equally busy. June, bless her, said that she would give the wedding reception at their home. Jim saw to all the legal side, the wedding licence etc., and drew up a remarkable table of times and arrangements for cars, in true army style. He was also a Territorial, a full Colonel, and he was made an A.D.C. to the Queen in the New Year's Honours, on the day before our wedding. Bernard was sent a copy and replied that Jim's orders were a masterpiece.

It was to be a very quiet wedding, no presents, no fuss, no dressing up, no guests except for close relatives. The time and place was twelve noon at St. Leonard's Church. Wilfred Westall, the Bishop of Crediton, helped by the Rector, married us and the famous Dr. Lionel Dakers, who was then organist at the Cathedral, played the organ as the regular St. Leonard's organist, poor man, was laid low with lumbago. My wedding dress was really nice. It was a lovely turquoise blue, thick ribbed, silk dress and full length coat to match, with a small hat in two shades of orchid pink.

The evening before the wedding I gave a little family party at the Rougemont Hotel, where we could have a private room and an open bar which was new to me, but which I thought was a very good idea. The bar was staffed by two white coated barmen. I told all my guests to ask for exactly what they wanted; it would be rung up on the till and the bill submitted to me in due course. Jim had arranged all this for me. I was most anxious for the Michelmores and Montgomerys to meet before the wedding. It was quite a small party, about thirty I suppose, and included Godwin's grandchildren of all ages who were supplied with soft drinks and plenty of crisps. I remember Bunty saying to me, 'How lucky you are having so many step grandchildren.'

Brian, Bunty, Margaret and I all slept at the Rougemont that night and early next morning Margaret and I ran along to the Cathedral for the early Communion service. It was very cold and snowing a little. The service was held in the tiny Oldham Chapel by the Reverend Harry Rann, who was going to be Bishop Westall's chaplain later that day and who had no idea that he was going to see me there at that hour. He said a special prayer for me and Godwin. Margaret and I ran back to our bedroom and a big breakfast tray and while we were eating the phone rang. It was Gary from Los Angeles! He had found out secretly from Godwin exactly where I would be. It was all so exciting. My two sisters-in-law saw that I was correctly dressed, then Brian said, 'We must all have a glass of champagne to settle Winsome.' Next came an excited hall porter knocking on the door and saying, 'Sir, your brother has arrived.' Bernard, the old warrior, had driven down from Bournemouth, where he was spending the winter. He was far too old and tired really to undertake such a journey, but he did. He came in a large black car with the Union Flag flying in front and the Chief Constable sent two motor cyclists to direct him into Exeter to the hotel and was there to greet him.

This was no quiet wedding; far from it. There were people all along the road and outside the church, television cameras and reporters, not only because of Monty, but also because it was such a romantic wedding of two old people! I think it took

Marriage to Godwin. With 'Monty', who gave me away. 1971

people's fancy in the dark cold winter. The church was packed to overflowing. The service was short and beautiful. We had to face a battery of cameras when we came out, but we finally got away and up to Westhay where warmth and a lovely lunch awaited us.

I was so very grateful to my dear old brother for coming such a long way in such cold weather. David, his son, could not come as he was skiing in Switzerland. He said to me later that our wedding killed his father. It was indeed his last social engagement, though he lived for another five years and I am sure it was one of his happiest days.

Godwin and I drove off after lunch to Torquay, for a happy five day honeymoon at the Imperial Hotel, staying in the Bridal Suite. On our way home, we broke our journey at Ashcombe Tower to have lunch with my dear friends Ralph and Betty Rayner. Such a wonderful idea of their's and then at last we were home in my new house.

Before describing that I will tell you about my new husband. He was very good looking, tall, six feet one and a half inches, broad, he weighed fourteen stone, with very thick silver hair, a close cut moustache and what all my women friends admired, twinkly eyes. He was great fun and loved to laugh. He was knighted in 1953, being made K.B.E., had been made C.B in 1945, held the D.S.O., M.C. and Territorial (Officers) Decoration. He was a Deputy Lieutenant and a magistrate, Chairman of Wonford Court. He had been a solicitor and had retired from being senior partner of Messrs. Michelmores just before I got to know him. He had also been Diocesan Registrar, the legal advisor to the Bishop, which entails many jobs in a large diocese. Naturally the Diocesan Registrar and the Bishop see a lot of each other and become friends.

The first bishop Godwin worked with was Lord William Cecil, whom the whole of Devon knew and loved. Next was Bishop Curzon, then Bishop Robert Mortimore, a brilliantly clever man who became a real friend of Godwin's. Godwin told me a funny story about his arrival in Exeter. It happened when Godwin was Mayor and therefore had to meet the new Bishop at a little ceremony in Broadgate. The Bishop had to give the

Mayor a gold sovereign but he had not got one on him and Godwin had to lend him one! He, the Bishop, used to visit us frequently. He had a charming way of inviting himself. He would telephone Godwin and say, 'May I come and pay my respects to Winsome this evening?' When he arrived I would settle the two men with their drinks, whisky for the Bishop, gin and vermouth for Godwin, and leave them to talk happily. I never sat with them, I just appeared to say goodbye when I heard the drawing room door open. It was a sad day when Bishop Mortimore retired to the North of England, so far away from Devon.

Our home, 10, St. Leonard's Road, was a charming old Georgian house with a pretty verandah along the front and all the rooms I could want. There was a collection of shops at the end of the road, affectionately known as 'the Village', where everybody was really friendly.

Godwin and I got to know each other more and more and kept discovering what a lot we had in common. His chief hobby was gardening. I carried on with my work at 'The Lodge' and for a year continued to go to London on the first Monday of the month. Later I gave it up and handed the job over to another member of the committee, because all day I worried about Godwin being alone, and all day he worried about me until I got home after half past six.

17

During the next eight years we led an interesting life. Twice Godwin took me to the Order of the Bath service in Westminster Abbey. followed by a little party with drinks in the garden of a house in Dean's Yard. Once, our first summer, we went to a Royal Garden Party at Buckingham Palace. On each occasion we spent a night at the Army and Navy Club, known to everyone in the Services as 'The Rag'. Godwin had been a member for years and I was made an Associate at once, the first time I had ever had a London club. It was in Pall Mall and very close to Buckingham Palace, so that we walked to the Garden Party, and indeed to Westminster Abbey also.

At the Garden Party we wondered if we would see anyone we knew amongst the thousands of guests. We did; we met one couple we knew and we saw an Exeter surgeon, Mr. Capener, being presented to the Duke of Edinburgh. We strolled about looking at everything with great interest. There were lots of Bishops attending, well known M.P.s and women in lovely summer clothes. One morning when we had spent two nights at 'The Rag' we went for a walk in the Mall and saw a rehearsal of the Trooping of the Colour with a beautiful woman rider taking the part of Her Majesty the Queen.

Every year in the summer we went on holiday somewhere different; once an unforgettable one to York. We loved that. We stayed in a very good hotel exactly opposite the West Front of the Minster and I used to slip over to half past five Evensong most days. We walked all round the wall of the city, taking a few days to do it, a bit at a time. We went to Durham, where I had always wanted to go, and across the Dales to Whitby by car, which Jim had thoughtfully ordered to be at our disposal; a real luxury.

One year we went on another unforgettable trip up the Rhine on a Botel, as it was called. We went to Amsterdam by boat from Harwich, having stayed the night before at 'The Rag'. We spent a few hours seeing the sights and then boarded the Botel. We had a very compact cabin, with a tiny bathroom, but it was quite adequate. All the staff were Danish university students, charming girls; and the food, largely Danish, was delicious. I was fascinated by the Rhine and all the places we passed; Mainz, Mannheim, Bonn, Cologne, the Lorelei Rock. I even enjoyed going through the industrial areas, factories and a poor quarter with barges on which whole families lived. It was so strange to see a pram on board and baby clothes hanging out to dry on a line. We made friends with a couple who had also spent the night at 'The Rag', Major General and Mrs. Blacker, and went everywhere as a foursome.

Another year we went on a narrow boat along a canal. The boat drifted along at a slow rate, through fields with a narrow footpath each side and locks to go through with enchanting lock houses. I wish I could remember where we started but I cannot! We drove up there from Exeter and we only went sixty miles in the week, ending up at Oxford where Kate, Jim's daughter, was at College. She met us and we took her out to dinner. Going from the simplicity of a canal to the sophistication of the Thames with grand boats and people sitting on wide decks, while we were on a boat measuring only seven feet, was a joke! Our cabin was the smallest place we had ever slept in; one bunk, a tiny little cupboard, a wee wash basin and the smallest shower I have ever seen. I thought Godwin would hate it, but he didn't. He loved it all. Sue, the wife of the skipper, Steve, cooked three course meals in her tiny galley; quite an education to watch her. It was a really restful holiday, 'far from the madding crowd'.

Twice, two years running, we went to Badminton for the Horse Trials. We stayed each time with a cousin of Godwin's who hunted with the Beaufort and so was able to get us excellent seats in the stand on the final day.

Another year we had a lovely holiday in Herefordshire in a hotel run by Godwin's daughter, Sue, and her husband Tim Harvey. We drove there and back, Godwin liked doing things comfortably. Of course we were getting older so were entitled to our comforts. I was seventy five and Godwin was seventy six when we married.

Then as we got older our holidays had to be near at hand, so we had two at Sidmouth and the last one at Exmouth. Godwin had had a slight stroke in the summer of 1979 and that slowed him up a lot.

My brother Bernard, the Field Marshal, died in 1976. We knew he was failing and I wanted to see him again, and to take Godwin to see him, at 'The Mill', his home near Alton. We drove there and back, having made careful plans with Pauline, his nurse, to ensure that he would see me. Very often he would suddenly say that he did not feel up to it and the unfortunate visitor would have to leave! General Sir Brian Horrocks was one of his most frequent visitors and I believe he was never turned away.

We arrived at half past two. Pauline and I went up to his room, Pauline going in and saying cheerfully, 'Well Sir, I have a visitor for you.' I heard Bernard's weak voice say, 'Who is it?' and I said, 'Winsome,' and walked boldly in. He looked very small and ill, but his blue eyes were as bright as ever and I think he was very pleased to see me. When I told him that Godwin was downstairs and asked if he would see him he said, 'No, I don't think so,' so I said no more for a while, then, 'You know Godwin would like to see you. Won't you let him just stand inside the door and say hello?' 'All right,' said my brother, 'call him up.' Godwin came at once and he and Bernard had a really nice chat together. I was so glad, for we never saw him again.

When he died there was, of course, a gathering of the clan for the big funeral. John and Dawn Montgomery of the Canadian branch (John is Donald's son) came over from Vancouver, Margaret came from Scotland and so on. We all spent the night before at the Basil Street Hotel and Godwin gave a dinner party for us.

Next morning, all dressed in deep black, we got into a fleet of cars and set off on the long drive to Windsor following the coffin. I shall never forget that coffin, with only the Union Jack and his famous beret on it. He was the first ever Field Marshal to go to his funeral without his baton, it had been stolen some years before when 'The Mill' was burgled in Bernard's absence from home. A baton is a personal present from the reigning monarch and Bernard's had been given to him by His Majesty King George VI. I am still haunted by the memory of that long drive. All along the route people were waiting to see him pass. We saw crowds in the various towns we went through, on the country roads we saw perhaps an old couple waiting or some farmers, who all took off their hats. Groups of soldiers drilling near Aldershot were called to form ranks in salute. Brian and Godwin were quite honestly in tears and as for me, I was drenched in tears. David, Tessa, Henry and Arabella were in the first car, Godwin and I, with Brian and Bunty were in the second.

When we reached Windsor it was too much for me. I have never seen such crowds, people on every pathway and wall, people hanging out of every window, all in dead silence. I must have looked very white, for when we got out of the cars and gathered on the green in front of the steps up to the Chapel, Tessa asked me if I was all right. 'No,' I said, 'I feel very shaky.' 'Then take this,' said Tessa, handing me a tiny green pill, 'and in twenty minutes you will feel all right.' I swallowed it at once and Tessa was right, soon I felt completely calm, able to face anything and I have never remembered to ask Tessa what that little pill was!

The service was very beautiful. The coffin was carried in by eight Guardsmen and the Pall Bearers were all Field Marshals, in full uniforms of course. Sir Richard Hull, our local, much loved Field Marshal, passed close to me. The Duke of Edinburgh represented the Queen. Immediately he left the Chapel, we, the family, followed him and photographs were taken of us as we went down the steps.

We got into more cars and drove to Binsted, the village where 'The Mill' is and where Bernard was to be buried. The same eight enormous Guardsmen carried him to the site of the grave which Bernard had chosen, under a tree at one side of the cemetery, and a thrush sang his heart out as the Vicar read the service.

Then there was a family luncheon at 'The Mill', after which we all went our various ways home. 'The Mill' is now the home of my beloved nephew David and Tessa his wife. The famous War Caravans have been given to the Imperial War Museum and David has greatly improved the garden, built on another room and a new and bigger kitchen. I love to go there. It is all so pretty now; it needed a woman's touch which Tessa, who is very artistic, has provided.

Amongst the many things I enjoyed with Godwin were the monthly concerts of the Bournemouth Symphony Orchestra held in the Great Hall of the University. Also we went to all the Mayoral functions, for Godwin had been Mayor of Exeter in 1949-50. That was the year when the Queen, then Princess Elizabeth, came to Exeter to open Princesshay and she lunched at the Guildhall. Godwin and Phoebe, his first wife, thoroughly enjoyed their mayoral life. When I married him, six years after Phoebe died, the City Council very kindly included me in the invitations to the annual dinners in the Guildhall. They were the first of such functions that I had ever attended. I did not know anything about Mayors or Guildhalls and I had quite a lot to learn, but I enjoyed meeting the Aldermen and Councillors, many of whom we already knew. Another smaller get together was The Twelve Club, a dinner club of twelve prominent business-men of Exeter. We met at different hotels or restaurants each year. Our life was busy and happy.

18

Then very suddenly Godwin had a stroke, though not a bad one. It hampered his speech to some extent and although that improved, his mouth always drooped slightly on one side. His left hand and leg were also affected so that he could not grip very hard and the leg frequently gave way, leading to many falls. Our doctor, Dr. Powell, foresaw that there would be problems and told me that we must move him downstairs to sleep before he had to be carried down.

June and Jim came to my rescue as they always did. June and I went out and bought an orthopaedic bed and moved down his big chest of drawers. In fact we made a bed sitting room out of the drawing room, still keeping sofa and armchairs as before, so that no one really felt it was a bedroom. Having a nice big cloakroom next door was a great help and when he had learned to use a Zimmer frame, Godwin could walk about to the dining room and into the garden. But he gradually deteriorated and nurses became a necessity. We had excellent ones and Godwin became very fond of them. I was always on duty from 2 p.m. to 6 p.m., then again after he had been put to bed.

Jim used to look in and see his father at least once a week and the two girls, June and Sue, at all times. Jo, the third of Godwin's family, lived in Australia. Godwin had had four children, an elder boy called Bill had died at the age of seven to the great and bitter grief of Phoebe and Godwin, of a congenital heart defect. Then came Jim, Jo who married Trevor, an Australian, and Sue who married Tim Harvey. They all had children and, as I write now, they too have had children, our great grandchildren. I do so enjoy still being part of a big happy family, having always been used to it from the first. Jo, nickname for Joan, came on holiday from Australia before Godwin became ill and again just before he died. I was so sorry for her, living so far away; it was hard on her.

Directly Godwin had the stroke, I realised that he would never be able to hold a razor so I said that he must grow a beard, which he did and delighted in telling everyone that he had now joined the Navy and become an Admiral! I kept it well trimmed and short and it was most becoming. He could use a battery razor a little when Tim gave him one. Of course there was no more gardening and that really was a blow, but dear Bridget Grant Watson, who looks after so many Exeter gardens, took us on and always conferred with Godwin before she did any big jobs.

In the summer of 1982 our life at No. 10 came to an end when Dr. Powell told us that Godwin was beyond being nursed at home and must go into a Nursing Home. It all happened very quickly. We got a nice room for him at the Argyll Nursing Home, facing fields with a glorious view, and moved him by ambulance as soon as we could. I will not write much about this; it was so pathetic to see Godwin's grief at leaving his home. He had wanted to die there. I too had to leave the house for I wanted to be with him all and every day and I could not live in a large empty house only at night. So I accepted the offer of a room from one of our nurses and moved into it, taking some furniture with me. Jim dealt with the house and all the furniture, which the children divided up between them. It was a good thing to do. I kept all I wanted, some lovely pictures and personal things, and the house was soon sold. Jim had thought that I would stay on, but I could not possibly ever contemplate it.

After about a month, Godwin took a turn for the worse. Everyone was very kind and the nurses gave me lunch and tea so that I could spend nearly all day with him. Mrs. Stockton, who had taken me in, drove me to and fro and took care of me. The Dean, Richard Eyre, was also very kind, visiting Godwin several times. He came on Saturday, October 23rd and gave him his final blessing and Godwin died on the evening of Monday, October 25th.

We had a beautiful funeral service in the Cathedral and then took him to Topsham to be buried in the family plot in the cemetery there, on October 29th. He was eighty eight. I do not remember much about anything for some time. I was numb.

I lived on in my furnished room for about ten months and I made a life for myself there, attending St. James's Church regularly, having visits from my friends and getting better all the time. I shall always be grateful for that interlude. Things have always turned out for the best for me. At last my 'landlady' needed my room and, after a rather anxious time as to where I would go next, June and I heard of a new block of flats for sale in Bartholomew Street West, by the old cemetery. We went to see them one Friday, were shown three from which to choose and selected one which had a wonderful view of Haldon and the City in front of it. June was a great help as she noticed everything, all the practical points, whereas I, in my excitement, might well have made a bad judgement! She went home to lunch to tell Jim I had made my choice. He went to see the Agent, put down the required deposit and bought the flat in my name.

I had a home again and great was the rejoicing. It was 'all hands on deck' from then on. Great measuring of furniture, choosing and ordering of carpets, curtains to be made and so on. Tim did a lot of carpentry work putting up towel rails, coat pegs etc., everything to make it comfortable. I bought some lovely little pieces of reproduction antique furniture, my own pictures and other furniture were installed, and I moved in on July 13th, 1983, one of the hottest days of the year.

From the start I was happy. My new next door neighbours called on me at once and so did another resident, so I made three lasting friends straight away and in no time got to know many of the other occupants. The block is called Homecourt House. It was not finished for some time while the builders in charge added more phases and laid out a garden. My little flat is delightful. It consists of a very sunny bedroom facing south-east with the most wonderful view of Exeter and Haldon which continues right round to Whitestone, which I can see from my sitting room windows. There are night storage heaters in both rooms and in the little hall. A lovely bathroom, a big cupboard, containing meters and a hot water tank, with lots of room for bed linen, cleaning things and all the junk which so quickly collects and which I call my glory hole, and a tiny but compact kitchen. Everything is electric so I only have one fuel bill.

The whole building is carpeted and heated. There is a lift, as well as stairs, but best of all there is a truly wonderful Warden who, with reliefs, is always on duty, day and night. Each room has an alarm bell to ring if we are in any difficulty and I suspect that they are rung more often than we know. People find they cannot get out of the bath, or are taken ill suddenly, but one ring of the bell and the Warden is there to take charge. We pay a maintenance bill for all that and pay it very gladly. There is also a large community lounge full of arm chairs and tables, very comfortable and sunny and a boon to people who want companions to talk to. Lots of friendships are made there, as they are also in the well fitted laundry room.

All the years that have passed have seen many of my family visiting me. Sheila and her husband Anton come twice a year for two nights at a time in the spring and autumn. Nowadays they stay with Jim and June, with whom they have made great friends. But only for the night, they spend the day with me and I revel in having them. Gary has been over from the United States twice to see me and then Henry, my dear great nephew, and Caroline, his wife, visit me regularly for lunch, coming down from their farm in North Devon. Now, to my enormous joy, they have a little daughter so that I have my first great great niece to visit me as well. She has been called Alexa Maud, Maud being my mother's name and my first name. She is, of course, the most beautiful baby in the world! Gary and I went to see them and we had a photograph taken of the four generations. I cannot entertain on any scale, I am too old, but I am still capable of having one guest at a time to what I call a trolley lunch and a great many people come to those. The Dean and his wife and the Bishop's wife are amongst my treasured guests. Sue comes to tea once a week, June also. Both girls keep a watchful eye on me, frequently telephoning to know how I am and if I want any shopping done.

Four generations. With Gary, Henry and Caroline and baby Alexa, my great, great niece. 1984

19

I am so happy, I love being alone. I have never minded that and I sometimes have a day when I see no one but just sit and think. There is so much to think about, after all I am very nearly ninety years of age. So much has happened in those years and so much has altered.

Life at New Park in Ireland, with a house full of family and friends was such fun. I remember the food particularly. We had a tradition that there would always be seven puddings on Sunday, who started it I do not know. It was always the same seven but we never got tired of them and we could ask for a mixture if we liked. They were banana custard, chocolate blancmange, delicious that, why do we not have it now? Junket, which Mother called curds and cream, jelly, which we called plonk, a bowl of fresh fruit, an apple or plum pie and perhaps a baked custard.

Food was plentiful at all our meals. At breakfast we began with porridge, which was eaten standing up and walking about, then a hot dish of something and always hot white and brown scones. The boys needed a good breakfast as they all went down to bathe in the icy cold lough every morning. That bathe would ease the pressure on the bathrooms. There were two of them, one called 'Meribah' ('. . . by the waters of Meribah we sat down and wept . . . .') which was Mother's and Father's. The other called 'Moab' (' . . . Moab is my wash pot . . . .') which was ours.

Father had names for all the rooms tacked up on their doors. At the top of the house there were two very big bedrooms, each with four beds, called 'Lombok' and 'Bali'. Father's study was up there too. The boys' room, with four or five beds, was 'The Zoo' and my room was 'The Hermit's Cell', it only had two beds.

We needed all these beds as we all invited our own guests and often sat down 18-21 for meals. No questions were asked, we just said who we would like to have. Mother and Father also invited tired clergy or perhaps an orphan child, all mixed in well and Mother organized the dates of arrival and departure. What a magical life we led. No wonder we loved New Park so much.

In the evenings we played games, Pitt, Up Jenkins, Happy Families, sang songs round the piano or acted charades. On Sunday evenings Mother always read aloud to us, perhaps 'The Scarlet Pimpernel' or another favourite was Tennyson's 'Enoch Arden', she had a beautiful reading voice. Occasionally we played Prisoner's Base or Sardines, all over the house, while our long suffering parents shut themselves into the Drawing Room.

There was a lot of ragging. We girls would frequently make apple pie beds or would sew up the legs of the boys' pyjamas. Loud were the curses when we did that! Another trick was to put holly under the bottom sheet and the boys would do the same to us.

On Sundays we always had sausages for breakfast. Then we would all gather in the hall properly dressed in suits and pretty dresses. After stopping in the garden to pick buttonholes, we went through a little gate into the churchyard. Over this gate was written, 'High is the gate thereof but the Door is low.' It would never have occurred to anyone that they should not go to church, we all went and we all loved it and bellowed out the hymns. There was an old fashioned organ which was pumped by Lizzie MacFarlane, who got redder and redder as the service went on.

After lunch we all went up to Father's study, sitting on the floor, overflowing everywhere, while he read us one of his 'Visions' for half an hour. Then everyone went for a long walk to settle our huge lunch and get up another appetite for tea, which was always hot toasted Sally Lunns. Two of us were detailed each week to toast and butter them and when Wangy and I were engaged tea was always late!

Wangy had the same adoration for my father that we all had. I would describe Father as being a humourous saint. He *was* a saint but he was a very human and humorous one. He had a fund of hilarious Irish stories, he was a great sportsman and a good shot. In his young days he was often asked to big shoots at Shane's Castle, the O'Neill's place, and he saw to it that all my brothers learned to shoot properly, he had their guns properly measured and he sent them to shoot clay pigeons. He had been a good cricketer, playing at Lords three years running for Harrow, but was never quite good enough to be captain. The Times was always seized upon every morning by my father and the boys to see what the latest scores were.

He cured me of being frightened by thunder in one fearsome storm when the whole lough was lit up by lightning and thunder roared. He insisted on me coming up to his study to watch it and held me in his arms whenever I burrowed by head into them. 'Listen,' he said, 'it's like God speaking,' and after that night I was never scared again. One magical night, from the same window, we saw the Northern Lights, but only once, I think that happened one August.

My father was a friend of Lord William Cecil, the Bishop of Exeter, and on one occasion when he came to Exeter to preach Mother came too. After dinner, while the Bishops lingered over their port, Mother and Lady Florence sat and discussed domestic affairs, in particular the long time it took to boil the kettle for their morning tea over a spirit lamp. 'If only the water wasn't so cold.' Mother said. 'Oh,' said Lady Florence, 'you should do what I do and tip the water out of the stone hot water bottle. It's extraordinary how warm it keeps all night.' I often remember that story as I boil my electric kettle to make an early cup of tea.

There have been so many changes in my lifetime. Take transport for instance. In my young days people went abroad by sea, in small or large steamers, all over the world, but now that form of travel is obsolete except for some expensive sea cruises.

Trains have run ever since I can remember, but were very different. The carriages were not heated as they are now, but by long metal containers filled with boiling water which were put in place just before the train started and which kept our feet beautifully warm. They would be changed at various stopping places. Then we had the loveliest lunch baskets, which were ordered in advance and brought along by a porter. These baskets were quite big and contained cold chicken, ham and salad, rolls and butter, plates, cutlery and napkins but I do not think there was any sort of drink.

In the towns, horse trams and horse buses were everywhere. Oh, the joy of getting on a London bus, drawn by two horses with the driver up on the top! I shall never forget the rush to get up onto the top deck so as to get one of the seats next to the driver. If he was friendly he would talk, pointing out places of interest to us with his long whip. There were thick leather 'rugs' to button over our knees on all the top seats.

When there was a 'pea soup' fog the driver had a tricky time. London fogs were bad due to all the coal burnt in homes and shops. Then there were runners sent out to help pedestrians, cabs and buses find their way and I can remember the eerie silence; every sound was muffled except for ghostly voices, 'Are you there?' 'Where are you?' People would carry torches. Another thing I remember is the habit of putting straw down on the road outside a house where anyone was ill so that the noise of horses' hooves would not worry the invalid. Very different to now when hooting cars and thundering lorries rush past hospitals and nursing homes.

I do not know when I last saw the lamplighter. It must have been when I was in my teens, I should think. We loved to watch for him coming down the street with his long pole and reaching up to turn on the gas. The muffin man lasted longer. He went around ringing a bell and calling out, 'Muffins and Crumpets!' He had them on a big tray which rested on a round pad on his head, so that he did not have to hold the tray. Mother would give us perhaps sixpence or a shilling, according to the number wanted, and we would rush out to buy them and then have lovely, hot, toasted muffins for tea. I am glad to see muffins in the shops again now.

Sweets and chocolates? Ah now, how cheap they were! Everything was bought by the farthing, halfpenny or penny. Farthing sugar sticks were our cheapest favourites. One penny bought a large Fry's chocolate cream bar which divided into four nice squares. Sherbet and liquorice sticks cost a penny as did large, black and white, peppermint balls. At Moville, in Ireland, one shop made and sold a particularly delicious toffee called 'Peggy's Leg', one penny a stick. We were often allowed to make toffee at home. Butter and sugar were cheap and it was quite usual to see large plates of syrupy toffee hardening in the nursery.

Desmond and I were a mercenary pair. When a visitor was due we would whisper to each other, 'Do you think he will give us a tip? If he does we can buy a lot of things and have a midnight feast.' We would lie awake until we thought all the household was asleep and then drag out and eat all the food we had hidden away. Greedy little pigs!

Most of all I think of all my family and also of my many dear friends. The oldest are dying off, I have very few old friends left, but I have so many young ones and I do like young people. I may say that sixty is young to me. I laugh to think that Sheila, my favourite girl, is now a grannie to eight little granddaughters and she is only about sixty three I believe.

People have sometimes asked me if I fear death. NO, I do not. I look forward to it. I have had the most wonderfully full, happy life and I do not want it to last much longer, but I am so grateful for all of it. When death comes, it will just be going on another journey to a land of which, as yet, I know nothing.

THE END

Exeter
19th January 1985